Puffin Books

RAMONA THE PEST

'Ramona started it,' said Howie. But then things always *did* start with Ramona, for she was a really high-voltage live wire, or, as her sister put it, a pest. Even on her long-awaited first day at school she was in trouble at once for asking awkward questions, for pulling good little Susan's fascinating curls, and for giving just a little snore to show her new teacher how very well she was resting when they all had to lie down on little mats. But *she* couldn't help it if all the others started to snore too, and then to giggle, so why did she get the blame?

The other days went much the same way. Still loving her teachers, still full of enthusiasm, Ramona always got up to something before it was time to go home for her tuna fish sandwiches. It might be hiding in the big children's school when a substitute teacher came to take her class, or walking so stickily deep in the mud on the building site that her feet couldn't move a step to get her to school, or just being 'the baddest witch' in the Hallowe'en parade, but whatever it was only Ramona would ever have thought of it.

Anyone who has ever found it a struggle to be good will love these observant, funny stories about poor Ramona, who really is quite a nice, funny child – so long, of course, as she's not *your* little sister, and with you *all* the time.

Beverly Cleary was born in Oregon, U.S.A., and lived in a town so small it had no library. Her mother arranged to have books sent and acted as librarian in a room over a bank, and there Mrs Cleary learned to love books. She spent much of her childhood either with books or on her way to and from the public library. After graduating from the University of California at Berkeley, and the School of Librarianship at Washington, she specialized in library work with children. The Clearys have grown-up twins, and live in California.

Beverly Cleary

Ramona the Pest

Illustrations by
Louis Darling

Puffin Books
in association with
Hamish Hamilton Children's Books

0140307745

PUFFIN BOOKS

Published by the Penguin Group
Penguin Books Ltd, 27 Wrights Lane, London W8 5TZ, England
Penguin Books USA Inc., 375 Hudson Street, New York, New York 10014, USA
Penguin Books Australia Ltd, Ringwood, Victoria, Australia
Penguin Books Canada Ltd, 10 Alcorn Avenue, Toronto, Ontario, Canada M4V 3B2
Penguin Books (NZ) Ltd, 182–190 Wairau Road, Auckland 10, New Zealand

Penguin Books Ltd, Registered Offices: Harmondsworth, Middlesex, England

First published in the USA 1968
First published in Great Britain by Hamish Hamilton 1974
Published in Puffin Books 1976
20 19 18 17 16

Printed in England by Clays Ltd, St Ives plc
Set in Monotype Baskerville

12.12.93

Contents

Chapter 1

Ramona's Great Day

'I am *not* a pest,' Ramona Quimby told her big sister Beezus.

'Then stop acting like a pest,' said Beezus, whose real name was Beatrice. She was standing by the front window waiting for her friend Mary Jane to walk to school with her.

'I'm not acting like a pest. I'm singing and skipping,' said Ramona, who had only recently learned to skip with both feet. Ramona did not think she was a pest. No matter what others said, she never thought she was a pest. The people who called her a pest were always bigger and so they could be unfair.

Ramona went on with her singing and skipping. 'This is a great day, a great day, a great day!' she sang, and to Ramona, who was feeling grown-up in a dress instead of play clothes, this was a great day, the greatest day of her whole life. No longer would she have to sit on her tricycle watching Beezus and Henry Huggins and the rest of the boys and girls in the neighbourhood go off to school. Today she was going to school, too. Today she was going to learn to read and write and do all the things that would help her catch up with Beezus.

'Come *on*, Mama!' urged Ramona, pausing in her singing and skipping. 'We don't want to be late for school.'

'Don't pester, Ramona,' said Mrs Quimby. 'I'll get you there in plenty of time.'

'I'm *not* pestering,' protested Ramona, who never meant to pester. She was not a slow-poke grown-up. She was a girl who could not wait. Life was so interesting she had to find out what happened next.

Then Mary Jane arrived. 'Mrs Quimby, would it

be all right if Beezus and I take Ramona to kindergarten?' she asked.

'No!' said Ramona instantly. Mary Jane was one of those girls who always wanted to pretend she was a mother and who always wanted Ramona to be the baby. Nobody was going to catch Ramona being a baby on her first day of school.

'Why not?' Mrs Quimby asked Ramona. 'You could walk to school with Beezus and Mary Jane just like a big girl.'

'No, I couldn't.' Ramona was not fooled for an instant. Mary Jane would talk in that silly voice she used when she was being a mother and take her by the hand and help her across the street, and everyone would think she really was a baby.

'Please, Ramona,' coaxed Beezus. 'It would be lots of fun to take you in and introduce you to the kindergarten teacher.'

'No!' said Ramona, and stamped her foot. Beezus and Mary Jane might have fun, but she wouldn't. Nobody but a genuine grown-up was going to take her to school. If she had to, she would make a great big noisy fuss, and when Ramona made a great big noisy fuss, she usually got her own way. Great big noisy fusses were often necessary when a girl was the youngest member of the family and the youngest person on her street.

'All right, Ramona,' said Mrs Quimby. 'Don't make a great big noisy fuss. If that's the way you

feel about it, you don't have to walk with the girls. I'll take you.'

'Hurry, Mama,' said Ramona happily, as she watched Beezus and Mary Jane go out the door. But when Ramona finally got her mother out of the house, she was disappointed to see one of her mother's friends, Mrs Kemp, approaching with her son Howie and his little sister Willa Jean, who was riding in a stroller. 'Hurry, Mama,' urged Ramona, not wanting to wait for the Kemps. Because their mothers were friends, she and Howie were expected to get along with one another.

'Hi, there!' Mrs Kemp called out, so of course Ramona's mother had to wait.

Howie stared at Ramona. He did not like having to get along with her any more than she liked having to get along with him.

Ramona stared back. Howie was a solid-looking boy with curly blond hair. ('Such a waste on a boy,' his mother often remarked.) The legs of his new jeans were turned up, and he was wearing a new shirt with long sleeves. He did not look the least bit excited about starting kindergarten. That was the trouble with Howie, Ramona felt. He never got excited. Straight-haired Willa Jean, who was interesting to Ramona because she was so sloppy, blew out a mouthful of wet biscuit crumbs and laughed at her cleverness.

'Today my baby leaves me,' remarked Mrs Quimby with a smile, as the little group proceeded down Klickitat Street towards Glenwood School.

Ramona, who enjoyed being her mother's baby, did not enjoy being called her mother's baby, especially in front of Howie.

'They grow up quickly,' observed Mrs Kemp.

Ramona could not understand why grown-ups always talked about how quickly children grew up. Ramona thought growing up was the slowest thing there was, slower even than waiting for Christmas to come. She had been waiting years just to get to kindergarten, and the last half hour was the slowest part of all.

When the group reached the intersection nearest Glenwood School, Ramona was pleased to see that Beezus's friend Henry Huggins was the traffic boy in charge of that particular corner. After Henry had led them across the street, Ramona ran off towards the kindergarten, which was a temporary wooden building with its own playground. Mothers and children were already entering the open door. Some of the children looked frightened, and one girl was crying.

'We're late!' cried Ramona. 'Hurry!'

Howie was not a boy to be hurried. 'I don't see any tricycles,' he said critically. 'I don't see any dirt to dig in.'

Ramona was scornful. 'This isn't nursery school. Tricycles and dirt are for nursery school.' Her own tricycle was hidden in the garage, because it was too babyish for her now that she was going to school.

Some big first-grade boys ran past yelling, 'Kindergarten babies! Kindergarten babies!'

'We are *not* babies!' Ramona yelled back, as she led her mother into the kindergarten. Once inside she stayed close to her. Everything was so strange,

and there was so much to see: the little tables and chairs; the row of cupboards, each with a different picture on the door; the play stove; and the wooden blocks big enough to stand on.

The teacher, who was new to Glenwood School, turned out to be so young and pretty she could not have been a grown-up very long. It was rumoured she had never taught school before. 'Hello, Ramona. My name is Miss Binney,' she said, speaking each syllable distinctly as she pinned Ramona's name to her dress. 'I am so glad you have come to kindergarten.' Then she took Ramona by the hand

and led her to one of the little tables and chairs. 'Sit here for the present,' she said with a smile.

A present! thought Ramona, and knew at once she was going to like Miss Binney.

'Good-bye, Ramona,' said Mrs Quimby. 'Be a good girl.'

As she watched her mother walk out the door, Ramona decided school was going to be even better than she had hoped. Nobody had told her she was going to get a present the very first day. What kind of present could it be, she wondered, trying to remember if Beezus had ever been given a present by her teacher.

Ramona listened carefully while Miss Binney showed Howie to a table, but all her teacher said was, 'Howie, I would like you to sit here.' Well! thought Ramona. Not everyone is going to get a present so Miss Binney must like me best. Ramona watched and listened as the other boys and girls arrived, but Miss Binney did not tell anyone else he was going to get a present if he sat in a certain chair. Ramona wondered if her present would be wrapped in fancy paper and tied with a ribbon like a birthday present. She hoped so.

As Ramona sat waiting for her present she watched the other children being introduced to Miss Binney by their mothers. She found two members of the morning kindergarten especially interesting. One was a boy named Davy, who was small, thin, and eager. He was the only boy in the class in short pants, and Ramona liked him at once. She liked him so much she decided she would like to kiss him.

The other interesting person was a big girl named Susan. Susan's hair looked like the hair on the girls in the pictures of the old-fashioned stories Beezus liked to read. It was reddish-brown and hung in curls like springs that touched her shoulders and bounced as she walked. Ramona had never seen such curls before. All the curly-haired girls she knew wore their hair short. Ramona put her hand to her own short straight hair, which was an ordinary brown, and longed to touch that bright springy hair. She longed to stretch one of those curls and watch it spring back. *Boing!* thought Ramona, making a mental noise like a spring on a television cartoon and wishing for thick, springy *boing-boing* hair like Susan's.

Howie interrupted Ramona's admiration of Susan's hair. 'How soon do you think we get to go out and play?' he asked.

'Maybe after Miss Binney gives me the present,' Ramona answered. 'She said she was going to give me one.'

'How come she's going to give you a present?' Howie wanted to know. 'She didn't say anything about giving me a present.'

'Maybe she likes me best,' said Ramona.

This news did not make Howie happy. He turned to the next boy, and said, '*She's* going to get a present.'

Ramona wondered how long she would have to sit there to get the present. If only Miss Binney understood how hard waiting was for her! When the last child had been welcomed and the last tearful mother had departed, Miss Binney gave a little talk about the rules of the kindergarten and showed the class the door that led to the bathroom. Next she assigned each person a little cupboard. Ramona's cupboard had a picture of a yellow duck on the door, and Howie's had a green frog. Miss Binney explained that their hooks in the cloakroom were marked with the same pictures. Then she asked the class to follow her quietly into the cloakroom to find their hooks.

Difficult though waiting was for her, Ramona did not budge. Miss Binney had not told her to get up and go into the cloakroom for her present. She had told her to sit for the present, and Ramona was going to sit until she got it. She would sit as if she were glued to the chair.

Howie scowled at Ramona as he returned from the cloakroom, and said to another boy, 'The teacher is going to give *her* a present.'

Naturally the boy wanted to know why. 'I don't know,' admitted Ramona. 'She told me that if I sat here I would get a present. I guess she likes me best.'

By the time Miss Binney returned from the cloakroom, word had spread around the classroom that Ramona was going to get a present.

Next Miss Binney taught the class the words of a puzzling song about 'the dawnzer lee light', which Ramona did not understand because she did not know what a dawnzer was. 'Oh, say, can you see by the dawnzer lee light,' sang Miss Binney, and Ramona decided that a dawnzer was another word for a lamp.

When Miss Binney had gone over the song several times, she asked the class to stand and sing it with her. Ramona did not budge. Neither did Howie and some of the others, and Ramona knew they were hoping for a present, too. Copycats, she thought.

'Stand up straight like good Americans,' said Miss Binney so firmly that Howie and the others reluctantly stood up.

Ramona decided she would have to be a good American sitting down.

'Ramona,' said Miss Binney, 'aren't you going to stand with the rest of us?'

Ramona thought quickly. Maybe the question was some kind of test, like a test in a fairy tale. Maybe Miss Binney was testing her to see if she could get her out of her seat. If she failed the test, she would not get the present.

'I can't,' said Ramona.

Miss Binney looked puzzled, but she did not insist that Ramona stand while she led the class through the dawnzer song. Ramona sang along with the others and hoped that her present came next, but when the song ended, Miss Binney made no mention of the present. Instead she picked up a book. Ramona decided that at last the time had come to learn to read.

Miss Binney stood in front of her class and began to read aloud from *Mike Mulligan and His Steam Shovel*, a book that was a favourite of Ramona's because, unlike so many books for her age, it was neither quiet and sleepy nor sweet and pretty. Ramona, pretending she was glued to her chair, enjoyed hearing the story again and listened quietly with the rest of the kindergarten to the story of Mike Mulligan's old-fashioned steam shovel, which proved its worth by digging the basement for the new town hall of Poppersville in a single day beginning at dawn and ending as the sun went down.

As Ramona listened a question came into her mind, a question that had often puzzled her about the books that were read to her. Somehow books always left out one of the most important things anyone would want to know. Now that Ramona was in school, and school was a place for learning, perhaps Miss Binney could answer the question. Ramona waited quietly until her teacher had finished the story, and then she raised her hand the way Miss Binney had told the class they should raise their hands when they wanted to speak in school.

Joey, who did not remember to raise his hand, spoke out. 'That's a good book.'

Miss Binney smiled at Ramona, and said, 'I like the way Ramona remembers to raise her hand when she has something to say. Yes, Ramona?'

Ramona's hopes soared. Her teacher had smiled at her. 'Miss Binney, I want to know – how did Mike Mulligan go to the bathroom when he was digging the basement of the town hall?'

Miss Binney's smile seemed to last longer than smiles usually last. Ramona glanced uneasily around and saw that others were waiting with interest for the answer. Everybody wanted to know how Mike Mulligan went to the bathroom.

'Well – ' said Miss Binney at last. 'I don't really know, Ramona. The book doesn't tell us.'

'I always wanted to know, too,' said Howie, without raising his hand, and others murmured in agreement. The whole class, it seemed, had been wondering how Mike Mulligan went to the bathroom.

'Maybe he stopped the steam shovel and climbed out of the hole he was digging and went to a service station,' suggested a boy named Eric.

'He couldn't. The book says he had to work as fast as he could all day,' Howie pointed out. 'It doesn't say he stopped.'

Miss Binney faced the twenty-nine earnest members of the kindergarten, all of whom wanted to know how Mike Mulligan went to the bathroom.

'Boys and girls,' she began, and spoke in her clear, distinct way. 'The reason the book does not tell us how Mike Mulligan went to the bathroom is that it is not an important part of the story. The story is about digging the basement of the town hall, and that is what the book tells us.'

Miss Binney spoke as if this explanation ended the matter, but the kindergarten was not convinced. Ramona knew and the rest of the class knew that knowing how to go to the bathroom *was* important. They were surprised that Miss Binney did not understand, because she had showed them the bathroom the very first thing. Ramona could see there were some things she was not going to learn in school, and along with the rest of the class she stared reproachfully at Miss Binney.

The teacher looked embarrassed, as if she knew she had disappointed her kindergarten. She recovered quickly, closed the book, and told the class that if they would walk quietly out to the playground she would teach them a game called Grey Duck.

Ramona did not budge. She watched the rest of the class leave the room and admired Susan's *boing-boing* curls as they bounced about her shoulders, but she did not stir from her seat. Only Miss Binney could unstick the imaginary glue that held her there.

'Don't you want to learn to play Grey Duck, Ramona?' Miss Binney asked.

Ramona nodded. 'Yes, but I can't.'

'Why not?' asked Miss Binney.

'I can't leave my seat,' said Ramona. When Miss Binney looked blank, she added, 'Because of the present.'

'What present?' Miss Binney seemed so genuinely puzzled that Ramona became uneasy. The teacher sat down in the little chair next to

Ramona's, and said, 'Tell me why you can't play Grey Duck.'

Ramona squirmed, worn out with waiting. She had an uneasy feeling that something had gone wrong someplace. 'I want to play Grey Duck, but you –' she stopped, feeling that she might be about to say the wrong thing.

'But I what?' asked Miss Binney.

'Well ... uh ... you said if I sat here I would get a present,' said Ramona at last, 'but you didn't say how long I had to sit here.'

If Miss Binney had looked puzzled before, she now looked baffled. 'Ramona, I don't understand –' she began.

'Yes, you did,' said Ramona, nodding. 'You told me to sit here for the present, and I have been sitting here ever since school started and you haven't given me a present.'

Miss Binney's face turned red and she looked so embarrassed that Ramona felt completely confused. Teachers were not supposed to look that way.

Miss Binney spoke gently. 'Ramona, I'm afraid we've had a misunderstanding.'

Ramona was blunt. 'You mean I don't get a present?'

'I'm afraid not,' admitted Miss Binney. 'You see

"for the present" means for now. I meant that I wanted you to sit here for now, because later I may have the children sit at different desks.'

'Oh.' Ramona was so disappointed she had nothing to say. Words were so puzzling. *Present* should mean a present just as *attack* should mean to stick tacks in people.

By now all the children were crowding around the door to see what had happened to their teacher. 'I'm so sorry,' said Miss Binney. 'It's all my fault. I should have used different words.'

'That's all right,' said Ramona, ashamed to have the class see that she was not going to get a present after all.

'All right, class,' said Miss Binney briskly. 'Let's go outside and play Grey Duck. You, too, Ramona.'

Grey Duck turned out to be an easy game, and Ramona's spirits recovered quickly from her disappointment. The class formed a circle, and the person who was 'it' tagged someone who had to chase him around the circle. If 'it' was caught before he got back to the empty space in the circle, he had to go into the centre of the circle, which was called the mush pot, and the person who caught him became 'it'.

Ramona tried to stand next to the girl with the

springy curls, but instead she found herself beside Howie. 'I thought you were going to get a present,' gloated Howie.

Ramona merely scowled and made a face at Howie, who was 'it', but quickly landed in the mush pot because his new jeans were so stiff they slowed him down. 'Look at Howie in the mush pot!' crowed Ramona.

Howie looked as if he were about to cry, which Ramona thought was silly of him. Only a baby would cry in the mush pot, Me, me, somebody tag me, thought Ramona, jumping up and down. She longed for a turn to run around the circle. Susan was jumping up and down, too, and her curls bobbed enticingly.

At last Ramona felt a tap on her shoulder. Her turn had come to run around the circle! She ran as fast as she could to catch up with the shoes pounding on the asphalt ahead of her. The *boing-boing* curls were on the other side of the circle. Ramona was coming closer to them. She put out her hand. She took hold of a curl, a thick, springy curl –

'*Yow!*' screamed the owner of the curls.

Startled, Ramona let go. She was so surprised by the scream that she forgot to watch Susan's curl spring back.

Susan clutched her curls with one hand and

pointed at Ramona with the other. 'That girl pulled my hair! That girl pulled my hair! Ow-ow-ow.' Ramona felt that Susan did not have to be so touchy. She had not meant to hurt her. She only wanted to touch that beautiful, springy hair that was so different from her own straight brown hair.

'Ow-ow-ow!' shrieked Susan, the centre of everyone's attention.

'Baby,' said Ramona.

'Ramona,' said Miss Binney, 'in our kindergarten we do not pull hair.'

'Susan doesn't have to be such a baby,' said Ramona.

'You may go sit on the bench outside the door while the rest of us play our game,' Miss Binney told Ramona.

Ramona did not want to sit on any bench. She wanted to play Grey Duck with the rest of the class. 'No,' said Ramona, preparing to make a great big noisy fuss. 'I won't.'

Susan stopped shrieking. A terrible silence fell over the playground. Everyone stared at Ramona in such a way that she almost felt as if she were beginning to shrink. Nothing like this had ever happened to her before.

'Ramona,' said Miss Binney quietly. 'Go sit on the bench.'

Without another word Ramona walked across the playground and sat down on the bench by the door of the kindergarten. The game of Grey Duck continued without her, but the class had not forgotten her. Howie grinned in her direction. Susan continued to look injured. Some laughed and pointed at Ramona. Others, particularly Davy, looked worried, as if they had not known such a terrible punishment could be given in kindergarten.

Ramona swung her feet and pretended to be watching some workmen who were building a new market across the street. In spite of the misunderstanding about the present, she wanted so much to be loved by her pretty new teacher. Tears came into Ramona's eyes, but she would not cry. Nobody was going to call Ramona Quimby a crybaby. Never.

Next door to the kindergarten two little girls, about two and four years old, peered solemnly through the fence at Ramona. 'See that girl,' said the older girl to her little sister. 'She's sitting there because she's been bad.' The two-year-old looked awed to be in the presence of such wickedness. Ramona stared at the ground, she felt so ashamed.

When the game ended, the class filed past

Ramona into the kindergarten. 'You may come in now, Ramona,' said Miss Binney pleasantly.

Ramona slid off the bench and followed the others. Even though she was not loved, she was forgiven, and that helped. She hoped that learning to read and write came next.

Inside Miss Binney announced that the time had come to rest. This news was another disappointment to Ramona, who felt that anyone who went to kindergarten was too old to rest. Miss Binney gave each child a mat on which there was a picture that matched the picture on his cupboard door and told him where to spread his mat on the floor. When all twenty-nine children were lying down they did not rest. They popped up to see what others were doing. They wiggled. They whispered. They coughed. They asked, 'How much longer do we have to rest?'

'Sh-h,' said Miss Binney in a soft, quiet, sleepy voice. 'The person who rests most quietly will get to be the wake-up fairy.'

'What's the wake-up fairy?' demanded Howie, bobbing up.

'Sh-h,' whispered Miss Binney. 'The wake-up fairy tiptoes around and wakes up the class with a magic wand. Whoever is the fairy wakes up the quietest resters first.'

Ramona made up her mind that she would get to be the wake-up fairy, and then Miss Binney would know she was not so bad after all. She lay flat on her back with her hands tight to her sides. The mat was thin and the floor was hard, but Ramona did not wiggle. She was sure she must be the best rester in the class, because she could hear others squirming around on their mats. Just to show Miss Binney she really and truly was resting she gave one little snore, not a loud snore but a delicate snore, to prove what a good rester she was.

A scatter of giggles rose from the class, followed by several snores, less delicate than Ramona's. They led to more and more, less and less delicate snores until everyone was snoring except the few who did not know how to snore. They were giggling.

Miss Binney clapped her hands and spoke in a voice that was no longer soft, quiet, and sleepy. 'All right, boys and girls!' she said. 'This is enough! We do not snore or giggle during rest time.'

'Ramona started it,' said Howie.

Ramona sat up and scowled at Howie. 'Tattletale,' she said in a voice of scorn. Across Howie she saw that Susan was lying quietly with her beautiful curls spread out on her mat and her eyes screwed tight shut.

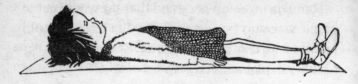

'Well, you did,' said Howie.

'Children!' Miss Binney's voice was sharp. 'We must rest so that we will not be tired when our mothers come to take us home.'

'Is your mother coming to take you home?' Howie asked Miss Binney. Ramona had been wondering the same thing.

'That's enough, Howie!' Miss Binney spoke the way mothers sometimes speak just before dinnertime. In a moment she was back to her soft, sleepy voice. 'I like the way Susan is resting so quietly,' she said. 'Susan, you may be the wake-up fairy and tap the boys and girls with this wand to wake them up.'

The magic wand turned out to be nothing but an everyday yardstick. Ramona lay quietly, but her efforts were of no use. Susan with her curls bouncing about her shoulders tapped Ramona last. It's not fair, Ramona thought. She was not the worst rester in the class. Howie was much worse.

The rest of the morning went quickly. The class was allowed to explore the paints and the toys, and those who wanted to were allowed to draw with their new crayons. They did not, however, learn to read and write, but Ramona cheered up when Miss Binney explained that anyone who had anything to share with the class could bring it to school the next day for Show and Tell. Ramona was glad when the bell finally rang and she saw her mother waiting for her outside the fence. Mrs Kemp and Willa Jean were waiting for Howie, too, and the five started home together.

Right away Howie said, 'Ramona got benched, and she's the worst rester in the class.'

After all that had happened that morning, Ramona found this too much. 'Why don't you shut up?' she yelled at Howie just before she hit him.

Mrs Quimby seized Ramona by the hand and dragged her away from Howie. 'Now Ramona,' she said, and her voice was firm, 'this is no way to behave on your first day of school.'

'Poor little girl,' said Mrs Kemp. 'She's worn out.'

Nothing infuriated Ramona more than having a grown-up say, as if she could not hear, that she was worn out. 'I'm *not* worn out!' she shrieked.

'She got plenty of rest while she was benched,' said Howie.

'Now Howie, you stay out of this,' said Mrs

Kemp. Then to change the subject, she asked her son, 'How do you like kindergarten?'

'Oh – I guess it's all right,' said Howie without enthusiasm. 'They don't have any dirt to dig in or tricycles to ride.'

'And what about you, Ramona?' asked Mrs Quimby. 'Did you like kindergarten?'

Ramona considered. Kindergarten had not turned out as she had expected. Still, even though she had not been given a present and Miss Binney did not love her, she had liked being with boys and girls her own age. She liked singing the song about the dawnzer and having her own little cupboard. 'I didn't like it as much as I thought I would,' she answered honestly, 'but maybe it will get better when we have Show and Tell.'

Chapter 2
Show and Tell

Ramona looked forward to many things – her first loose tooth, riding a bicycle instead of a tricycle, wearing lipstick like her mother – but most of all she looked forward to Show and Tell. For years Ramona had watched her sister Beezus leave for school with a doll, a book, or a pretty leaf to share with her class. She had watched Beezus's friend Henry Huggins carry mysterious, lumpy packages past her house on his way to school. She had listened to Beezus talk about the interesting things her class brought to school – turtles, ballpoint pens that wrote in three different colours, a live clam in a jar of sand and seawater.

Now at last the time had come for Ramona to show and tell. 'What are you going to take to show your class?' she asked Beezus, hoping for an idea for herself.

'Nothing,' said Beezus, and went on to explain. 'Along about the third grade you begin to outgrow Show and Tell. By the fifth grade it's all right to take something really unusual like somebody's pickled appendix or something to do with social studies. An old piece of fur when you study fur traders would be all right. Or if something really exciting happened like your house burning down, it would be all right to tell about that. But in the fifth grade you don't take an old doll or a toy fire engine to school. And you don't call it Show and Tell by then. You just let the teacher know you have something interesting.'

Ramona was not discouraged. She was used to Beezus's growing out of things as she grew into them. She rummaged around in her toy box and finally dragged out her favourite doll, the doll with the hair that could really be washed. 'I'm going to take Chevrolet,' she told Beezus.

'Nobody names a doll Chevrolet,' said Beezus, whose dolls had names like Sandra or Patty.

'I do,' Ramona answered. 'I think Chevrolet is the most beautiful name in the world.'

'Well, she's a horrid-looking doll,' said Beezus. 'Her hair is green. Besides, you don't play with her.'

'I wash her hair,' said Ramona loyally, 'and the only reason what's left of her hair looks sort of green is that I tried to blue it like Howie's grandmother, who has her hair blued at the beauty shop. Mama said putting bluing on yellow hair turned it green. Anyway, I think it's pretty.'

When the time finally came to start to school, Ramona was disappointed once more to see Mrs Kemp approaching with Howie and little Willa Jean. 'Mama, come *on*,' begged Ramona, dragging at her mother's hand, but her mother waited until the Kemps had caught up. Willa Jean was even sloppier this morning. There were crumbs on the front of her sweater, and she was drinking apple juice out of a nursing bottle. Willa Jean dropped the bottle when she saw Chevrolet and sat there with apple juice dribbling down her chin while she stared at Ramona's doll.

'Ramona is taking her doll to school for Show and Tell,' said Mrs Quimby.

Howie looked worried. 'I don't have anything for Show and Tell,' he said.

'That's all right, Howie,' said Mrs Quimby. 'Miss Binney doesn't expect you to take something every day.'

'I *want* to take something,' said Howie.

'My goodness, Howie,' said his mother. 'What if twenty-nine children each brought something. Miss Binney wouldn't have time to teach you anything.'

'*She's* taking something.' Howie pointed to Ramona.

There was something familiar about the way Howie was behaving. Ramona pulled at her mother's hand. 'Come *on*, Mama.'

'Ramona, I think it would be nice if you ran in the house and found something to lend Howie to take to school,' said Mrs Quimby.

Ramona did not think this idea was nice at all, but she recognized that lending Howie something might be faster than arguing with him. She ran into the house where she snatched up the first thing she saw – a stuffed rabbit that had already been given hard wear before the cat had adopted it as a sort of practice mouse. The cat liked to chew the rabbit's tail, carry it around in his mouth, or lie down and kick it with his hind feet.

When Ramona thrust the rabbit into Howie's hand, Mrs Kemp said, 'Say thank you, Howie.'

'It's just an old beat-up bunny,' said Howie scornfully. When his mother wasn't looking, he handed the rabbit to Willa Jean, who dropped her apple juice, seized the rabbit, and began to chew its tail.

Just like our cat, thought Ramona, as the group proceeded towards school.

'Don't forget Ramona's bunny,' said Mrs Kemp, when they reached the kindergarten playground.

'I don't want her old bunny,' said Howie.

'Now Howie,' said his mother. 'Ramona was kind enough to share her bunny so you be nice.' To Mrs Quimby she said, as if Howie could not hear, 'Howie needs to learn manners.'

Share! Ramona had learned about sharing in nursery school, where she either had to share something of her own that she did not want to share or she had to share something that belonged to someone else that she did not want to share either. 'That's all right, Howie,' she said. 'You don't have to share my rabbit.'

Howie looked grateful, but his mother thrust the rabbit into his hands anyway.

At the beginning, on that second day of kindergarten, Ramona felt shy because she was not sure

what Miss Binney would think about a girl who had
been made to sit on the bench. But Miss Binney
smiled, and said, 'Good morning, Ramona,' and
seemed to have forgotten all about the day before.
Ramona sat Chevrolet in her little cupboard with
the duck on the door and waited for Show and Tell.

'Did anyone bring something to show the class?'
asked Miss Binney, after the class had sung the
dawnzer song.

Ramona remembered to raise her hand, and
Miss Binney invited her to come to the front of the
room to show the class what she had brought.
Ramona took Chevrolet from her cupboard and
stood beside Miss Binney's desk, where she discovered she did not know what to say. She looked to
Miss Binney for help.

Miss Binney smiled encouragingly. 'Is there
something you would like to tell us about your
doll?'

'I can really wash her hair,' said Ramona. 'It's
sort of green because I gave her a blue rinse.'

'And what do you wash it with?' asked Miss
Binney.

'Lots of things,' said Ramona, beginning to enjoy
speaking in front of the class. 'Soap, shampoo, de-
tergent, bubble bath. I tried Dutch Cleanser once,
but it didn't work.'

'What is your doll's name?' asked Miss Binney.

'Chevrolet,' answered Ramona. 'I named her after my aunt's car.'

The class began to laugh, especially the boys. Ramona felt confused, standing there in front of twenty-eight boys and girls who were all laughing at her. 'Well, I did!' she said angrily, almost tearfully. Chevrolet was a beautiful name, and there was no reason to laugh.

Miss Binney ignored the giggles and snickers. 'I think Chevrolet is a lovely name,' she said. Then she repeated, 'Chev-ro-let.' The way Miss Binney pronounced the word made it sound like music. 'Say it, class.'

'Chev-ro-let,' said the class obediently, and this time no one laughed. Ramona's heart was filled with love for her teacher. Miss Binney was not like most grown-ups. Miss Binney understood.

The teacher smiled at Ramona. 'Thank you, Ramona, for sharing Chevrolet with us.'

After a girl had showed her doll that talked when she pulled a cord in its back and a boy had told the class about his family's new refrigerator, Miss Binney asked, 'Does anyone else have anything to show us or tell us about?'

'That boy brought something,' said Susan of the springy curls, pointing at Howie.

Boing, thought Ramona, as she always did when
those curls caught her attention. She was beginning
to see that Susan was a girl who liked to take
charge.

'Howie, did you bring something?' asked Miss
Binney.

Howie looked embarrassed.

'Come on, Howie,' encouraged Miss Binney.
'Show us what you brought.'

Reluctantly Howie went to his cupboard and
brought out the shabby blue rabbit with the damp
tail. He carried it to Miss Binney's desk, faced the
class, and said in a flat voice, 'It's just an old
bunny.' The class showed very little interest.

'Is there something you would like to tell us
about your bunny?' asked Miss Binney.

'No,' said Howie. 'I just brought it because my
mother made me.'

'I can tell you something about your bunny,' said Miss Binney. 'It has had lots of love. That's why it's so worn.'

Ramona was fascinated. In her imagination she could see the cat lying on the carpet with the rabbit gripped in his teeth while he battered it with his hind feet. The look that Howie gave the rabbit was somehow lacking in love. Ramona waited for him to say that it wasn't his rabbit, but he did not. He just stood there.

Miss Binney, seeing that Howie could not be encouraged to speak in front of the class, opened a drawer in her desk, and as she reached inside she said, 'I have a present for your bunny.' She pulled out a red ribbon, took the rabbit from Howie, and tied the ribbon around its neck in a bright bow. 'There you are, Howie,' she said. 'A nice new bow for your bunny.'

Howie mumbled, 'Thank you,' and as quickly as possible hid the rabbit in his cupboard.

Ramona was delighted. She felt that the red ribbon Miss Binney had given her old rabbit took the place of the present she had not been given the day before. All morning she thought about the things she could do with that red ribbon. She could use it to tie up what was left of Chevrolet's hair. She could trade it to Beezus for something valuable, an empty perfume bottle or some coloured paper that wasn't scribbled on. During rest time Ramona had the best idea of all. She would save the ribbon until she got a two-wheeled bicycle. Then she would weave it in and out of the spokes and ride so fast the ribbon would be a red blur as the wheels went around. Yes. That was exactly what she would do with her red ribbon.

When the noon bell rang, Mrs Quimby, Mrs Kemp, and little Willa Jean were waiting by the fence. 'Howie,' Mrs Kemp called out, 'don't forget Ramona's bunny.'

'Oh, that old thing,' muttered Howie, but he returned to his cupboard while Ramona walked along behind the mothers.

'Howie needs to learn responsibility,' Mrs Kemp was saying.

When Howie had caught up, he untied the ribbon and shoved the rabbit at Ramona. 'Here. Take your old rabbit,' he said.

Ramona took it and said, 'Give me my ribbon.'

'It's not your ribbon,' said Howie. 'It's my ribbon.'

The two mothers were so busy talking about

their children needing to learn responsibility they paid no attention to the argument.

'It is not!' said Ramona. 'It's my ribbon!'

'Miss Binney gave it to me.' Howie was so calm and so sure that he was right that Ramona was infuriated. She grabbed for the ribbon, but Howie held it away from her.

'Miss Binney tied it around my rabbit's neck so it's *my* ribbon!' she said, her voice rising.

'No,' said Howie flatly and calmly.

'Ribbons aren't for boys,' Ramona reminded him. 'Now give it to me!'

'It isn't yours.' Howie showed no excitement, only stubbornness.

Howie's behaviour drove Ramona wild. She wanted him to get excited. She wanted him to get angry. 'It is too mine!' she shrieked, and at last the mothers turned around.

'What's going on?' asked Mrs Quimby.

'Howie has my ribbon and won't give it back,' said Ramona, so angry she was near tears.

'It isn't hers,' said Howie.

The two mothers exchanged glances. 'Howie, where did you get that ribbon?' asked Mrs Kemp.

'Miss Binney gave it to me,' said Howie.

'She gave it to *me*,' corrected Ramona, as she

fought back tears. 'She tied it on my rabbit's neck, so it's my ribbon.' Anybody should be able to understand that. Anybody who was not stupid.

'Now Howie,' said his mother. 'What does a big boy like you want with a ribbon?'

Howie considered this question as if his mother really expected an answer. 'Well . . . I could tie it on the tail of a kite if I had a kite.'

'He just doesn't want me to have it,' explained Ramona. 'He's selfish.'

'I am not selfish,' said Howie. 'You want something that doesn't belong to you.'

'I do *not*!' yelled Ramona.

'Now Ramona,' said her mother. 'A piece of ribbon isn't worth all this fuss. We have other ribbons at home that you can have.'

Ramona did not know how to make her mother understand. No other ribbon could possibly take the place of this one. Miss Binney had given her the ribbon, and she wanted it because she loved Miss Binney so much. She wished Miss Binney were here now because her teacher, unlike the mothers, would understand. All Ramona could say was, 'It's mine.'

'I know!' said Mrs Kemp, as if a brilliant idea had come to her. 'You can share the ribbon.'

Ramona and Howie exchanged a look in which

they agreed that nothing would be worse than sharing the ribbon. They both knew there were some things that could never be shared, and Miss Binney's ribbon was one of them. Ramona wanted that ribbon, and she wanted it all to herself. She knew that a grubby boy like Howie would probably let Willa Jean drool on it and ruin it.

'That's a good idea,' agreed Mrs Quimby. 'Ramona, you let Howie carry it half-way home, and then you can carry it the rest of the way.'

'Then who gets it?' asked Howie, voicing the question that had risen in Ramona's thoughts.

'We can cut it in two so you each may have half,' said Mrs Kemp. 'We're having lunch at Ramona's house, and as soon as we get there we'll divide the ribbon.'

Miss Binney's beautiful ribbon chopped in two! This was too much. Ramona burst into tears. Her half would not be long enough for anything. If she ever got a two-wheeled bicycle, there would not be enough ribbon to weave through the spokes of a wheel. There would not even be enough to tie up Chevrolet's hair.

'I'm tired of sharing,' said Howie. 'Share, share, share. That's all grown-ups ever talk about.'

Ramona could not understand why both mothers were amused by Howie's words. She understood exactly what Howie meant, and she liked him a little better for saying so. She had always had a guilty feeling she was the only person who felt that way.

'Now Howie, it isn't as bad as all that,' said his mother.

'It is too,' said Howie, and Ramona nodded through her tears.

'Give me the ribbon,' said Mrs Kemp. 'Maybe after lunch we'll all feel better.'

Reluctantly Howie surrendered the precious ribbon, and said, 'I suppose we're having tuna-fish sandwiches again.'

'Howie, that's not polite,' said his mother.

At the Quimbys' house, Ramona's mother said, 'Why don't you and Howie play with your tricycle while I prepare lunch?'

'Sure, Ramona,' said Howie, as the two mothers boosted Willa Jean's stroller up the steps, and he and Ramona were left together whether they wanted to be or not. Ramona sat down on the steps and tried to think of a name to call Howie. Pieface wasn't bad enough. If she used some of the names she had heard big boys use at school, her mother would come out and scold her. Perhaps 'little booby boy' would do.

'Where's your trike?' asked Howie.

'In the garage,' answered Ramona. 'I don't ride it anymore now that I'm in kindergarten.'

'How come?' asked Howie.

'I'm too big,' said Ramona. 'Everybody else on the street rides two-wheelers. Only babies ride tricycles.' She made this remark because she knew Howie still rode his tricycle, and she was so angry about the ribbon she wanted to hurt his feelings.

If Howie's feelings were hurt, he did not show it. He seemed to be considering Ramona's remarks in his usual deliberate way. 'I could take off one of the wheels if I had some pliers and a screwdriver,' he said at last.

Ramona was indignant. 'And wreck my tricycle?' Howie just wanted to get her into trouble.

'It wouldn't wreck it,' said Howie. 'I take the wheels off my tricycle all the time. You can ride on the front wheel and one back wheel. That way you'd have a two-wheeler.'

Ramona was not convinced.

'Come on, Ramona,' coaxed Howie. 'I like to take wheels off tricycles.'

Ramona considered. 'If I let you take off a wheel, do I get to keep the ribbon?'

'Well . . . I guess so.' After all, Howie was a boy. He was more interested in taking a tricycle apart than he was in playing with any ribbon.

Ramona was doubtful about Howie's ability to turn her tricycle into a two-wheeler, but she was determined to have Miss Binney's red ribbon.

She trundled her tricycle out of the garage. Then she found the pliers and a screwdriver, and handed them to Howie, who went to work in a businesslike way. He used the screwdriver to pry off the hub. With the pliers he straightened the cotter pin that held the wheel in place, removed it from the axle, and pulled off the wheel. Next he returned the cotter pin to its hole in the axle and bent the ends out once more so the axle would stay in place. 'There,' he said with satisfaction. For once he looked happy and sure of himself 'You have to sort of lean to one side when you ride it.'

Ramona was so impressed by Howie's work that her anger began to drain away. Maybe Howie was right. She grasped her tricycle by the handlebars and mounted the seat. By leaning towards the side on which the wheel had been removed, she managed to balance herself and to ride down the driveway in an uncertain and lopsided fashion. 'Hey! It works!' she called out, when she reached the pavement. She circled and pedalled back towards Howie, who stood beaming at the success of his alteration.

'I told you it would work,' he bragged.

'I didn't believe you at first,' confessed Ramona, who would never again be seen riding a babyish three-wheeler.

The back door opened, and Mrs Quimby called out, 'Come on, children. Your tuna sandwiches are ready.'

'See my two-wheeler,' cried Ramona, pedalling in a lopsided circle.

'Well, aren't you a big girl!' exclaimed her mother. 'How did you ever manage to do that?'

Ramona came to a halt. 'Howie fixed my trike for me and told me how to ride it.'

'What a clever boy!' said Mrs Quimby. 'You must be very good with tools.'

Howie beamed with pleasure at this compliment.

'And Mama,' said Ramona, 'Howie says I can have Miss Binney's ribbon.'

'Sure,' agreed Howie. 'What do I want with an old ribbon?'

'I'm going to weave it in and out of the front spokes of my two-wheeler and ride so fast it will make a blur,' said Ramona. 'Come on, Howie, let's go eat our tuna-fish sandwiches.'

Chapter 3
Seat Work

There were two kinds of children who went to kindergarten – those who lined up beside the door before school, as they were supposed to, and those who ran around the playground and scrambled to get into line when they saw Miss Binney approaching. Ramona ran around the playground.

One morning as Ramona was running around the playground she noticed Davy waiting for Henry Huggins to lead him across the intersection. She was interested to see that Davy was wearing a black cape pinned to his shoulders with two big safety pins.

While Henry held up two cars and a cement truck, Ramona watched Davy crossing the street. The more Ramona saw of Davy, the better she liked him. He was such a nice shy boy with blue eyes and soft brown hair. Ramona always tried to choose Davy for her partner in folk dancing, and when the class played Grey Duck Ramona always tagged Davy unless he was already in the mush pot.

When Davy arrived, Ramona marched up to him, and asked, 'Are you Batman?'

'No,' said Davy.

'Are you Superman?' asked Ramona.

'No,' said Davy.

Who else could Davy be in a black cape? Ramona stopped and thought, but was unable to think of anyone else who wore a cape. 'Well, who are you?' she asked at last.

'Mighty Mouse!' crowed Davy, delighted that he had baffled Ramona.

'I'm going to kiss you, Mighty Mouse!' shrieked Ramona.

Davy began to run and Ramona ran after him. Round and round the playground they ran with Davy's cape flying out behind him. Under the travelling bars and around the jungle gym she chased him.

'Run, Davy! Run!' screamed the rest of the class, jumping up and down, until Miss Binney was seen approaching, and everyone scrambled to get into line.

Every morning afterwards when Ramona reached the playground she tried to catch Davy so she could kiss him.

'Here comes Ramona!' the other boys and girls shouted, when they saw Ramona walking down the street. 'Run, Davy! Run!'

And Davy ran with Ramona after him. Round and round the playground they ran while the class cheered Davy on.

'That kid ought to go out for track when he gets a little older,' Ramona heard one of the workmen across the street say one day.

Once Ramona came near enough to grab Davy's clothes, but he jerked away, popping the buttons off his shirt. For once Davy stopped running. 'Now see what you did!' he accused. 'My mother is going to be mad at you.'

Ramona stopped in her tracks. 'I didn't do anything,' she said indignantly. 'I just hung on. You did the pulling.'

'Here comes Miss Binney,' someone called out,

and Ramona and Davy scurried to get in line by the door.

After that Davy stayed farther away from Ramona than ever, which made Ramona sad because Davy was *such* a nice boy and she did so long to kiss him. However, Ramona was not so sad that she stopped chasing Davy. Round and round they went every morning until Miss Binney arrived.

Miss Binney, by this time, had begun to teach her class something more than games, the rules of the kindergarten, and the mysterious dawnzer song. Ramona thought of kindergarten as being divided

into two parts. The first part was the running part, which included games, dancing, finger painting, and playing. The second part was called seat work. Seat work was serious. Everyone was expected to work quietly in his own seat without disturbing anyone else. Ramona found it difficult to sit still, because she was always interested in what everyone else was doing. 'Ramona, keep your eyes on your own work,' Miss Binney said, and sometimes Ramona remembered.

For the first seat-work assignment each member of the class was told to draw a picture of his own house. Ramona, who had expected to learn to read and write in school like her sister Beezus, used her new crayons quickly to draw her house with two windows, a door, and a red chimney. With her green crayon she scrubbed in some shrubbery. Anyone familiar with her neighbourhood could tell the picture was of her house, but somehow Ramona was not satisfied. She looked around to see what others were doing.

Susan had drawn a picture of her house and was adding a girl with *boing-boing* curls looking out the window. Howie, who had drawn his house with the garage door open and a car inside, was adding a motorcycle parked at the kerb. Davy's house looked like a club-house built by some boys who had a few old boards and not enough nails. It leaned to one side in a tired sort of way.

Ramona studied her own drawing and decided she would have to do something to make it more interesting. After considering various colours of crayon, she selected the black and drew big black swirls coming from the windows.

'You aren't supposed to scribble on your picture,' said Howie, who also was inclined to pay attention to other people's work.

Ramona was indignant. 'I didn't scribble. The black is part of my picture.'

When Miss Binney asked the class to set their pictures on the chalk rail so that everyone might see them, the class noticed Ramona's picture at once, because it was drawn with bold, heavy strokes and because of the black swirls.

'Miss Binney, Ramona scribbled all over her house,' said Susan, who by now had revealed herself as the kind of girl who always wanted to play house so she could be the mother and boss everybody.

'I did not!' protested Ramona, beginning to see that her picture was going to be misunderstood by everyone. Maybe she had been wrong to try to make it interesting. Maybe Miss Binney did not want interesting pictures.

'You did too!' Joey ran up to the chalk rail and pointed to Ramona's black swirls. 'See!'

The class, including Ramona, waited for Miss Binney to say Ramona should not scribble on her picture, but Miss Binney merely smiled and said. 'Remember your seat, Joey. Ramona, suppose you tell us about your picture.'

'I didn't scribble on it,' said Ramona.

'Of course you didn't,' Miss Binney said.

Ramona loved her teacher even more. 'Well,' she began, 'that black isn't scribbling. It's smoke coming out of the windows.'

'And why is smoke coming out of the windows?' gently pressed Miss Binney.

'Because there's a fire in the fireplace and the chimney is stopped up,' explained Ramona. 'It's stopped up with Santa Claus, but he doesn't show in the picture.' Ramona smiled shyly at her teacher. 'I wanted to make my picture interesting.'

Miss Binney returned her smile. 'And you did make it interesting.'

Davy looked worried. 'How does Santa Claus get out?' he asked. 'He doesn't stay in there, does he?'

'Of course he gets out,' said Ramona. 'I just didn't show that part.'

The next day seat work got harder. Miss Binney said that everyone had to learn to print his name. Ramona saw right away that this business of names was not fair. When Miss Binney handed each member of the class a strip of cardboard with his name printed on it, anyone could see that a girl named Ramona was going to have to work harder than a girl named Ann or a boy named Joe. Not that Ramona minded having to work harder – she was eager to learn to read and write. Having been the youngest member of her family and of the neighbourhood, however, she had learned to watch for unfair situations.

Carefully Ramona printed *R* the way Miss Binney had printed it. *A* was easy. Even a baby could print *A*. Miss Binney said *A* was pointed like a witch's hat, and Ramona was planning to be a witch for the Hallowe'en parade. *O* was also easy. It was a round balloon. Some people's *O's* looked like leaky balloons, but Ramona's *O's* were balloons full of air.

'I like the way Ramona's *O's* are fat balloons full of air,' Miss Binney said to the class, and Ramona's heart filled with joy. Miss Binney liked her *O's* best!

Miss Binney walked around the classroom looking over shoulders. 'That's right, boys and girls. Nice pointed *A's*,' she said. '*A's* with nice sharp peaks. No, Davy. *D* faces the other way. Splendid, Karen. I like the way Karen's *K* has a nice straight back.'

Ramona wished she had a *K* in her name, so that she could give it a nice straight back. Ramona enjoyed Miss Binney's descriptions of the letters of the alphabet and listened for them while she worked. In front of her Susan played with a curl while she worked. She twisted it around her finger, stretched it out, and let it go. *Boing*, thought Ramona automatically.

'Ramona, let's keep our eyes on our work,' said Miss Binney. 'No, Davy. *D* faces the *other* way.'

Once more Ramona bent over her paper. The hardest part of her name, she soon discovered, was getting the right number of points on the *M* and *N*. Sometimes her name came out RANOMA. But before long she remembered that two points came first. 'Good work, Ramona,' said Miss Binney, the first time Ramona printed her name correctly. Ramona hugged herself with happiness and love for Miss Binney. Soon, she was sure, she would be able to join her letters together and write her name in the same rumply grown-up way that Beezus wrote her name.

Then Ramona discovered that some boys and girls had an extra letter followed by a dot. 'Miss Binney, why don't I have a letter with a dot after it?' she asked.

'Because we have only one Ramona,' said Miss Binney. 'We have two Erics. Eric Jones and Eric Ryan. We call them Eric J. and Eric R., because we don't want to get our Erics mixed up.'

Ramona did not like to miss anything. 'Could I have another letter with a little dot?' she asked,

ERIC J.   ERIC R.

knowing that Miss Binney would not think she was pestering.

Miss Binney smiled and leaned over Ramona's table. 'Of course you may. This is the way to make a *Q*. A nice round *O* with a little tail like a cat. And there is your little dot, which is called a full stop.' Then Miss Binney walked on, supervising seat work.

Ramona was charmed by her last initial. She drew a nice round *O* beside the one Miss Binney had drawn, and then she added a tail before she leaned back to admire her work. She had one balloon and two Hallowe'en hats in her first name and a cat in her last name. She doubted if anyone else in the morning kindergarten had such an interesting name.

The next day at seat-work time Ramona practised her *Q* while Miss Binney walked around helping those with *S* in their names. All the *S*'s were having trouble. 'No, Susan,' said Miss Binney. '*S* stands up straight. It does not lie down as if it were a little worm crawling along the ground.'

Susan pulled out a curl and let it spring back.

Boing, thought Ramona.

'My, how many *S*'s we have that are crawling along like little worms,' remarked Miss Binney.

Ramona was pleased that she had escaped *S*. She drew another *Q* and admired it a moment before she added two little pointed ears, and then she added two whiskers on each side so that her *Q* looked the way the cat looked when crouched on a rug in front of the fireplace. How pleased Miss Binney would be! Miss Binney would say to the kindergarten, 'What a splendid *Q* Ramona has made. It looks exactly like a little cat.'

'No, Davy,' Miss Binney was saying. 'A *D* does not have four corners. It has two corners. One side is curved like a robin redbreast.'

This conversation was so interesting that Ramona was curious to see Davy's *D* for herself.

She waited until Miss Binney had moved away before she slipped out of her seat and over to the next table to look at Davy's *D*. It was a great disappointment. 'That *D* doesn't look like a robin,' she whispered. 'It doesn't have any feathers. A robin has to have feathers.' She had watched robins pulling worms out of her front lawn many times. They all had feathers on their breasts, little soft feathers mussed by the wind.

Davy studied his work. Then he scrubbed out half his *D* with his eraser and drew it in a series of little jags. It did not look like Miss Binney's *D*, but it did look, in Ramona's opinion, more like the front of a robin with feathers mussed by the wind, which was what Miss Binney wanted, wasn't it? A *D* like a robin redbreast.

'Good work, Davy,' said Ramona, trying to sound like her teacher. Now maybe Davy would let her kiss him.

'Ramona,' said Miss Binney, 'in your seat, please.' She walked back to look at Davy's seat work. 'No, Davy. Didn't I tell you the curve of a *D* is as smooth as a robin redbreast? Yours is all jagged.'

Davy looked bewildered. 'Those are feathers,' he said. 'Feathers like a robin.'

'Oh, I'm sorry, Davy. I didn't mean ...' Miss

Binney behaved as if she did not know quite what to say. 'I didn't mean you to show each feather. I meant you to make it smooth and round.'

'Ramona told me to do it this way,' said Davy. 'Ramona said a robin has to have feathers.'

'Ramona is not the kindergarten teacher.' Miss Binney's voice, although not exactly cross, was not her usual gentle voice. 'You make your *D* the way I showed you and never mind what Ramona says.'

Ramona felt confused. Things had such an unexpected way of turning out all wrong. Miss Binney said a *D* should look like a robin redbreast, didn't she? And robins had feathers, didn't they! So why wasn't putting feathers on a *D* all right?

Davy glared at Ramona as he took his eraser and scrubbed out half his *D* a second time. He scrubbed so hard he rumpled his paper. 'Now see what you did,' he said.

Ramona felt terrible. Dear little Davy whom she loved so much was angry with her, and now he would run faster than ever. She never would get to kiss him.

And even worse, Miss Binney did not like *D's* with feathers, so she probably would not like *Q's* with ears and whiskers either. Hoping her teacher would not see what she was doing, Ramona quickly and regretfully erased the ears and whiskers from her *Q*. How plain and bare it looked with only its tail left to keep it from being an *O*. Miss Binney, who could understand that Santa Claus in the chimney would make a fireplace smoke, might be disappointed if she knew Ramona had given her *Q* ears and whiskers because lettering was different from drawing pictures.

Ramona loved Miss Binney so much she did not want to disappoint her. Not ever. Miss Binney was the nicest teacher in the whole world.

Chapter 4
The Substitute

Before long Mrs Quimby and Mrs Kemp decided the time had come for Ramona and Howie to walk to school by themselves. Mrs Kemp, pushing Willa Jean in her stroller, walked Howie to the Quimbys' house where Ramona's mother invited her in for a cup of coffee.

'You better put all your stuff away,' Howie advised Ramona, as his mother lifted his little sister out of the stroller. 'Willa Jean crawls around and chews things.'

Grateful for this advice, Ramona closed the door of her room.

'Now Howie, you be sure to look both ways before you cross the street,' cautioned his mother.

'You too, Ramona,' said Mrs Quimby. 'And be sure you walk. And walk on the pavement. Don't go running out in the street.'

'And cross between the white lines,' said Mrs Kemp.

'And wait for the traffic boy near the school,' said Mrs Quimby.

'And don't talk to strangers,' said Mrs Kemp.

Ramona and Howie, weighed down by the responsibility of walking themselves to school, trudged off down the street. Howie was even gloomier than usual, because he was the only boy in the morning kindergarten who wore jeans with only one hip pocket. All the other boys had two hip pockets.

'That's silly,' said Ramona, still inclined to be impatient with Howie. If Howie did not like his jeans, why didn't he make a great big noisy fuss about them?

'No, it isn't,' contradicted Howie. 'Jeans with one hip pocket are babyish.'

At the cross street Ramona and Howie stopped and looked both ways. They saw a car coming a block away so they waited. They waited and waited. When the car finally passed, they saw another car coming a block away in the opposite direction. They waited some more. At last the coast was clear, and they walked, stiff-legged in their haste, across the street. 'Whew!' said Howie, relieved that they were safely across.

The next intersection was easier because Henry Huggins, in his red traffic sweater and yellow cap, was the traffic boy on duty. Ramona was not awed by Henry even though he often got to hold up cement and lumber trucks delivering material for the market that was being built across from the school. She had known Henry and his dog Ribsy as long as she could remember, and she admired Henry because not only was he a traffic boy, he also delivered papers.

Now Ramona looked at Henry, who was standing with his feet apart and his hands clasped behind his back. Ribsy was sitting beside him as if he were watching traffic, too. Just to see what Henry would do, Ramona stepped off the kerb.

'You get back on the kerb, Ramona,' Henry ordered above the noise of the construction on the corner.

Ramona set one foot back on the kerb.

'All the way, Ramona,' said Henry.

Ramona stood with both heels on the kerb, but her toes out over the gutter. Henry could not say she

was not standing on the kerb, so he merely glared. When several boys and girls were waiting to cross the street, Henry marched across with Ribsy prancing along beside him.

'Beat it, Ribsy,' said Henry between his teeth. Ribsy paid no attention.

Directly in front of Ramona Henry executed a sharp about-face like a real soldier. Ramona marched behind Henry, stepping as close to his shoes as she could. The other children laughed.

On the opposite kerb Henry tried to execute another military about-face, but instead he tripped over Ramona. 'Doggone you, Ramona,' he said angrily. 'If you don't cut that out I'm going to report you.'

'Nobody reports kindergarteners,' scoffed an older boy.

'Well, I'm going to report Ramona if she doesn't cut it out,' said Henry. Obviously Henry felt it was his bad luck that he had to guard an intersection where Ramona crossed the street.

Between crossing the street without a grown-up and getting so much attention from Henry, Ramona felt that her day was off to a good start. However, as she and Howie approached the kindergarten building, she saw at once that something was wrong. The door to the kindergarten was already open. No one was playing on the jungle gym. No one was running around the playground. No one was even waiting in line by the door. Instead the boys and girls were huddled in groups like frightened mice. They all looked worried and once in a while someone who appeared to be acting brave would run to the open door, peer inside, and come running back to one of the groups to report something.

'What's the matter?' asked Ramona.

'Miss Binney isn't there,' whispered Susan. 'It's a different lady.'

'A substitute,' said Eric R.

Miss Binney not there! Susan must be wrong. Miss Binney had to be there. Kindergarten would not be kindergarten without Miss Binney. Ramona ran to the door to see for herself. Susan was right. Miss Binney was not there. The woman who was busy at Miss Binney's desk was taller and older. She was as old as a mother. Her dress was brown and her shoes were sensible.

Ramona did not like what she saw at all, so she ran back to a cluster of boys and girls. 'What are we going to do?' she asked, feeling as if she had been deserted by Miss Binney. For her teacher to go home and not come back was not right.

'I think I'll go home,' said Susan.

Ramona thought this idea babyish of Susan. She had seen what happened to boys and girls who ran home from kindergarten. Their mothers marched them straight back again, that's what happened. No, going home would not do.

'I bet the substitute won't even know the rules of our kindergarten,' said Howie.

The children agreed. Miss Binney said following the rules of their kindergarten was important. How could this stranger know what the rules were? A stranger would not even know the names of the boys and girls. She might get them mixed up.

Still feeling that Miss Binney was disloyal to stay away from school, Ramona made up her mind she was not going into that kindergarten room with that strange teacher. Nobody could make her go in there. But where could she go? She could not go home, because her mother would march her back. She could not go into the main building of Glenwood School, because everyone would know a girl her size belonged out in the kindergarten. She had to hide, but where?

When the first bell rang, Ramona knew she did not have much time. There was no place to hide on the kindergarten playground, so she slipped around behind the little building and joined the boys and girls who were streaming into the red-brick building.

'Kindergarten baby!' a first grader shouted at Ramona.

'Pieface!' answered Ramona with spirit. She could see only two places to hide – behind the bicycle racks or behind a row of trash cans. Ramona chose the trash cans. As the last children entered the building she got down on her hands and knees and crawled into the space between the cans and the red-brick wall.

The second bell rang. 'Hup, two, three, four! Hup, two, three, four!' The traffic boys were marching back from their posts at the intersections near the school. Ramona crouched motionless on the asphalt. 'Hup, two, three, four!' the traffic boys,

heads up, eyes front, marched past the trash cans and into the building. The playground was quiet, and Ramona was alone.

Henry's dog Ribsy, who had followed the traffic boys as far as the door of the school, came trotting over to check the odours of the trash cans. He put his nose down to the ground and whiffled around the cans while Ramona crouched motionless with the rough asphalt digging into her knees. Ribsy's busy nose led him around the can face to face with Ramona.

'Wuf!' said Ribsy.

'Ribsy, go away!' ordered Ramona in a whisper.

'R-r-r-wuf!' Ribsy knew Ramona was not supposed to be behind the trash cans.

'You be quiet!' Ramona's whisper was as ferocious as she could make it. Over in the kindergarten the class began to sing the song about the dawnzer. At least the strange woman knew that much about kindergarten. After the dawnzer song the kindergarten was quiet. Ramona wondered if the teacher knew that Show and Tell was supposed to come next. She strained her ears, but she could not hear any activity in the little building.

The space between the brick wall and the trash cans began to feel as cold as a refrigerator to

Ramona in her thin sweater. The asphalt dug into her knees, so she sat down with her feet straight out towards Ribsy's nose. The minutes dragged by.

Except for Ribsy, Ramona was lonely. She leaned against the chill red bricks and felt sorry for herself. Poor little Ramona, all alone except for Ribsy, behind the trash cans. Miss Binney would be sorry if she knew what she had made Ramona do. She would be sorry if she knew how cold and lonesome Ramona was. Ramona felt so sorry for the poor shivering little child behind the trash cans that one tear and then another slid down her cheeks. She sniffed pitifully. Ribsy opened one eye and looked at her before he closed it again. Not even Henry's dog cared what happened to her.

After a while Ramona heard the kindergarten running and laughing outside. How disloyal everyone was to have so much fun when Miss Binney had deserted her class. Ramona wondered if the kindergarten missed her and if anyone else would chase Davy and try to kiss him. Then Ramona must have dozed off, because the next thing she knew recess time had come and the playground was swarming with shouting, yelling, ball-throwing older boys and girls. Ribsy was gone. Stiff with cold, Ramona hunched down as low as she could. A ball bounced with a bang against a trash can. Ramona shut her eyes and hoped that if she could not see anyone, no one could see her.

Footsteps came running towards the ball. 'Hey!' exclaimed a boy's voice. 'There's a little kid hiding back here!'

Ramona's eyes flew open. 'Go away!' she said fiercely to the strange boy, who was peering over the cans at her.

'What are you hiding back there for?' asked the boy.

'*Go away!*' ordered Ramona.

'Hey, Huggins!' yelled the boy. 'There's a little kid back here who lives over near you!'

In a moment Henry was peering over the trash cans at Ramona. 'What are you doing there?' he demanded. 'You're supposed to be in kindergarten.'

'You mind your own business,' said Ramona.

Naturally when two boys peered behind the trash cans, practically the whole school had to join them to see what was so interesting. 'What's she doing?' people asked. 'How come she's hiding?' 'Does her teacher know she's here?'

In the midst of all the excitement, Ramona felt a new discomfort.

'Find her sister,' someone said. 'Get Beatrice. She'll know what to do.'

No one had to find Beezus. She was already there. 'Ramona Geraldine Quimby!' she said. 'You come out of there this minute!'

'I won't,' said Ramona, even though she knew she could not stay there much longer.

'Ramona, you just wait until Mother hears about this!' stormed Beezus. 'You're really going to catch it!'

Ramona knew that Beezus was right, but catching it from her mother was not what was worrying her at the moment.

'Here comes the yard teacher,' someone said.

Ramona had to admit defeat. She got to her hands and knees and then to her feet and faced the crowd across the trash can lids as the yard teacher came to investigate the commotion.

'Don't you belong in kindergarten?' the yard teacher asked.

'I'm not going to go to kindergarten,' said Ramona stubbornly, and cast an anguished glance at Beezus.

'She's supposed to be in kindergarten,' said Beezus, 'but she needs to go to the bathroom.' The older boys and girls thought this remark was funny, which made Ramona so angry she wanted to cry. There was nothing funny about it at all, and if she didn't hurry –

The yard teacher turned to Beezus. 'Take her to the bathroom and then to the principal's office. She'll find out what the trouble is.'

The first words were a relief to Ramona, but the second a shock. No one in the morning kindergarten had ever been sent to Miss Mullen's office in the big building, except to deliver a note from Miss Binney, and then the children went in pairs, because the errand was such a scary one. 'What will the principal do to me?' Ramona asked, as Beezus led her away to the girls' bathroom in the big building.

'I don't know,' said Beezus. 'Talk to you, I guess or call Mother. Ramona, why did you have to go and do a dumb thing like hiding behind the trash cans?'

'Because.' Ramona was cross since Beezus was so cross. When the girls came out of the bathroom, Ramona reluctantly allowed herself to be led into the principal's office, where she felt small and frightened even though she tried not to show it.

'This is my little sister Ramona,' Beezus explained to Miss Mullen's secretary in the outer office. 'She belongs in kindergarten, but she's been hiding behind the trash cans.'

Miss Mullen must have overheard, because she came out of her office. Frightened though she was,

Ramona braced herself to say, I won't go back to kindergarten!

'Why, hello, Ramona,' said Miss Mullen. 'That's all right, Beatrice. You may go back to your class. I'll take over.'

Ramona wanted to stay close to her sister, but Beezus walked out of the office, leaving her alone with the principal, the most important person in the whole school. Ramona felt small and pitiful with her knees still marked where the asphalt had gouged her. Miss Mullen smiled, as if Ramona's behaviour was of no particular importance, and said, 'Isn't it too bad Miss Binney had to stay home with a sore throat? I know what a surprise it was for you to find a strange teacher in your kindergarten room.'

Ramona wondered how Miss Mullen knew so much. The principal did not even bother to ask what Ramona was doing behind the trash cans. She did not feel the least bit sorry for the poor little girl with the gouged knees. She simply took Ramona by the hand, and said, 'I'm going to introduce you to Mrs Wilcox. I know you're going to like her,' and started out the door.

Ramona felt a little indignant, because Miss Mullen did not demand to know why she had been hiding all that time. Miss Mullen did not even notice how forlorn and tearstained Ramona looked. Ramona had been so cold and lonely and miserable that she thought Miss Mullen should show some interest. She had half expected the principal to say, Why you poor little thing! Why were you hiding behind the trash cans?

The looks on the faces of the morning kindergarten, when Ramona walked into the room with the principal, made up for Miss Mullen's lack of concern. Round eyes, open mouths, faces blank with surprise – Ramona was delighted to see the whole class staring at her from their seats. *They* were worried about her. *They* cared what had happened to her.

'Ramona, this is Miss Binney's substitute, Mrs Wilcox,' said Miss Mullen. To the substitute she said, 'Ramona is a little late this morning.' That was all. Not a word about how cold and miserable Ramona had been. Not a word about how brave she had been to hide until recess.

'I'm glad you're here, Ramona,' said Mrs Wilcox, as the principal left. 'The class is drawing with crayons. What would you like to draw?'

Here it was seat-work time, and Mrs Wilcox was not even having the class do real seat work, but was letting them draw pictures as if this day were the first day of kindergarten. Ramona was most disapproving. Things were not supposed to be this way. She looked at Howie scrubbing away with a blue crayon to make a sky across the top of his paper and at Davy, who was drawing a man whose arms seemed to come out of his ears. They were busy and happy drawing whatever they pleased.

'I would like to make *Q's*,' said Ramona on sudden inspiration.

'Make use of what?' asked Mrs Wilcox, holding out a sheet of drawing paper.

Ramona had been sure all along that the substitute could not be as smart as Miss Binney, but at least she expected her to know what the letter *Q* was. All grown-ups were supposed to know *Q*. 'Nothing,' Ramona said, as she accepted the paper and, pleasantly self-conscious under the awed stares of the kindergarten, went to her seat.

At last Ramona was free to draw her *Q* her own way. Forgetting the loneliness and discomfort of the morning, she drew a most satisfying row of *Q's*, Ramona-style, and decided that having a substitute teacher was not so bad after all.

Mrs Wilcox wandered up and down the aisle looking at pictures. 'Why, Ramona,' she said, pausing by Ramona's desk, 'what charming little cats you've drawn! Do you have kittens at home?'

Ramona felt sorry for poor Mrs Wilcox, a grown-up lady teacher who did not know *Q*. 'No,' she answered. 'Our cat is a boy cat.'

Chapter 5
Ramona's Engagement Ring

'No!' said Ramona on the first rainy morning after she had started kindergarten.

'Yes,' said Mrs Quimby.

'No!' said Ramona. 'I won't!'

'Ramona, be sensible,' said Mrs Quimby.

'I don't want to be sensible,' said Ramona. 'I hate being sensible!'

'Now, Ramona,' said her Mother, and Ramona knew she was about to be reasoned with. 'You have a new raincoat. Boots cost money, and Howie's old boots are perfectly good. The soles are scarcely worn.'

'The tops aren't shiny,' Ramona told her mother. 'And they're brown boots. Brown boots are for boys.'

'They keep your feet dry,' said Mrs Quimby, 'and that is what boots are for.'

Ramona realized she looked sulky, but she could not help herself. Only grown-ups would say boots were for keeping feet dry. Anyone in kindergarten knew that a girl should wear shiny red or white boots on the first rainy day, not to keep her feet dry, but to show off. That's what boots were for – showing off, wading, splashing, stamping.

'Ramona,' said Mrs Quimby sternly. 'Get that look off your face this instant. Either you wear these boots or you stay home from school.'

Ramona recognized that her mother meant what she said, and so, because she loved kindergarten, she sat down on the floor and dragged on the hated brown boots, which did not go with her new flowered plastic raincoat and hat.

Howie arrived in a yellow raincoat that was long enough for him to grow into for at least two years and a yellow rain hat that almost hid his face. Beneath the raincoat Ramona glimpsed a pair of shiny brown boots, which she supposed she would have to wear someday when they were old and dull and dirty.

'Those are my old boots,' said Howie, looking at Ramona's feet as they started off to school.

'You better not tell anybody.' Ramona plodded along on feet almost too heavy to lift. It was a perfect morning for anyone with new boots. Enough rain had fallen in the night to fill the gutters with muddy streams and to bring worms squirming out of the lawns on to the sidewalks.

The intersection by the school was unusually

quiet that morning, because rain had halted construction on the new market. Ramona was so downhearted that she did not even tease Henry Huggins when he led her across the street. The kindergarten playground, as she had expected, was swarming with boys and girls in raincoats, most of them too big, and boots, most of them new. The girls wore various sorts of raincoats and red or white boots – all except Susan, who carried her new white boots so she would not get them muddy. The boys looked alike, because they all wore yellow raincoats and hats and brown boots. Ramona was not even sure which boy was Davy, not that he mattered to her this morning. Her feet felt too heavy for chasing anyone.

Part of the class had lined up properly by the door, waiting for Miss Binney, while the rest ran about clomping, splashing, and stamping.

'Those are boy's boots you're wearing,' said Susan to Ramona.

Ramona did not answer. Instead she picked up a smooth pink worm that lay wiggling on the playground and, without really thinking, wound it around her finger.

'Look!' yelled Davy from beneath his big rain hat. 'Ramona's wearing a ring made out of a *worm!*'

Ramona had not thought of the worm as a ring until now, but she saw at once that the idea was interesting. 'See my ring!' she shouted, thrusting her fist towards the nearest face.

Boots were temporarily forgotten. Everyone ran screaming from Ramona to avoid being shown her ring.

'See my ring! See my ring!' shouted Ramona, racing around the playground on feet that were suddenly much lighter.

When Miss Binney appeared around the corner, the class scrambled to line up by the door. 'Miss Binney! Miss Binney!' Everyone wanted to be the first to tell. 'Ramona is wearing a worm for a ring!'

'It's a pink worm,' said Ramona, thrusting out her hand. 'Not an old dead white worm.'

'Oh ... what a pretty worm,' said Miss Binney bravely. 'It's so smooth and ... pink.'

Ramona elaborated. 'It's my engagement ring.'

'Who are you engaged to?' asked Ann.

'I haven't decided,' answered Ramona.

'Not me,' Davy piped up.

'Not me,' said Howie.

'Not me,' said Eric R.

'Well ... a ... Ramona ...' Miss Binney was searching for words. 'I don't think you should wear your ... ring during kindergarten. Why don't you put it down on the playground in a puddle so that it will ... stay fresh.'

Ramona was happy to do anything Miss Binney wanted her to. She unwound the worm from her finger and placed it carefully in a puddle, where it lay limp and still.

After that Ramona raced around the playground with a worm around her finger whenever her mother made her wear Howie's old boots to school, and when everyone asked who she was engaged to, she always answered, 'I haven't decided.'

'Not me!' Davy always said, followed by Howie, Eric R., and any other boy who happened to be near.

Then one Saturday Mrs Quimby examined

Ramona's scuffed shoes and discovered that not only were the heels worn down, the leather of the toes was worn through because Ramona stopped her lopsided two-wheeled tricycle by dragging her toes on the concrete. Mrs Quimby had Ramona stand up while she felt her feet through the leather.

'It's time for new shoes,' Mrs Quimby decided. 'Get your jacket and your boots, and we'll drive down to the shopping centre.'

'It isn't raining today,' said Ramona. 'Why do I have to take boots?'

'To see if they will fit over your new shoes,' answered her mother. 'Hurry along, Ramona.'

When they reached the shoe store, Ramona's favourite shoe salesman said, as Ramona and her mother sat down, 'What's the matter with my little Petunia today? Don't you have a smile for me?'

Ramona shook her head and looked sadly and longingly at a row of beautiful shiny girls' boots displayed on one side of the store. There she sat with Howie's dingy old brown boots beside her. How could she smile? A babyish nursery-school girl, who was wearing new red boots, was rocking joyously on the shoe store's rocking horse while her mother paid for the boots.

'Well, we'll see what we can do for you,' said the salesman briskly, as he pulled off Ramona's shoes and made her stand with her foot on the measuring stick. Finding the right pair of shoes for her did not take him long.

'Now try on the boots,' said Mrs Quimby in her no-nonsense voice, when Ramona had walked across the shoe store and back in her new shoes.

For a moment, as Ramona sat down on the floor and grasped one of the hated boots, she considered pretending she could not get it on. However, she knew she could not get away with this trick, because the shoe-store man understood both children and shoes. She pulled and yanked and tugged and managed to get her foot most of the way in. When she stood up she was on tiptoe inside the boot. Her mother tugged some more, and her shoe went all the way into the boot.

'There,' said Mrs Quimby. Ramona sighed.

The babyish nursery-school girl stopped rocking long enough to announce to the world, 'I have new boots.'

'Tell me, Petunia,' said the shoe man. 'How many boys and girls in your kindergarten?'

'Twenty-nine,' said Ramona with a long face. Twenty-nine, most of them with new boots. The happy booted nursery-school baby climbed off the rocking horse, collected her free balloon, and left with her mother.

The shoe man spoke to Mrs Quimby. 'Kindergarten teachers like boots to fit loosely so the children can manage by themselves. I doubt if Petunia's teacher has time to help with fifty-eight boots.'

'I hadn't thought of that,' said Mrs Quimby. 'Perhaps we had better look at boots after all.'

'I'll bet Petunia here would like red boots,' said the shoe man. When Ramona beamed, he added, 'I had a hunch that would get a smile out of you.'

When Ramona left the shoe store with beautiful red boots, *girl's* boots, in a box, which she carried herself, she was so filled with joy she set her balloon free just to watch it sail over the parking lot and up, up into the sky until it was a tiny red dot against the grey clouds. The stiff soles of her new shoes made such a pleasant noise on the pavement that she began to prance. She was a pony. No she was one of the three Billy Goats Gruff, the littlest one, trip-trapping over the bridge that the troll was hiding under. Ramona trip-trapped joyfully all the way to the parked car, and when she reached home she trip-trapped up and down the hall and all around the house.

'For goodness' sake, Ramona,' said Mrs Quimby,

while she was marking Ramona's name in the new boots, 'can't you just walk?'

'Not when I'm the littlest Billy Goat Gruff,' answered Ramona, and trip-trapped down the hall to her room.

Unfortunately, there was no rain the next morning so Ramona left her new boots at home and trip-trapped to school, where she did not have much chance of catching Davy because he could run faster than she could trip-trap in her stiff new shoes. She trip-trapped to her seat, and later, because she was art monitor who got to pass out drawing paper, she trip-trapped to the supply cupboard and trip-trapped up and down the aisles passing out paper.

'Ramona, I would like it if you walked quietly,' said Miss Binney.

'I am the littlest Billy Goat Gruff,' explained Ramona. 'I have to trip-trap.'

'You may trip-trap when we go outdoors.' Miss Binney's voice was firm. 'You may not trip-trap in the classroom.'

At playtime the whole class turned into Billy Goats Gruff and trip-trapped around the playground, but none so joyfully or so noisily as Ramona. The gathering clouds, Ramona noticed, were dark and threatening.

Sure enough, that evening rain began to fall, and all night long it beat against the south side of the Quimbys' house. The next morning Ramona, in her boots and raincoat, was out long before Howie arrived to walk to school with her. She waded through the wet lawn, and her boots became even shinier when they were wet. She stamped in all the little puddles on the driveway. She stood in the gutter and let muddy water run over the toes of her beautiful new boots. She gathered wet leaves to dam the gutter, so she could stand in deeper water. Howie, as she might have expected, was used to his boots and not a bit excited. He did enjoy stamping in puddles, however, and together they stamped and splashed on the way to school.

Ramona came to a halt at the intersection guarded by Henry Huggins in his yellow raincoat, rain hat, and brown boots. 'Look at all that nice mud,' she said, pointing to the area that was to be the parking lot for the new market. It was such nice mud, rich and brown with puddles and little rivers in the tyre tracks left by the construction trucks. It was the best mud, the muddiest mud, the most tempting mud Ramona had ever seen. Best of all, the day was so rainy there were no construction workers around to tell anyone to stay out of the mud.

'Come on, Howie,' said Ramona. 'I'm going to see how my boots work in the mud.' Of course, she would get her shiny boots muddy, but then she could have the fun of turning the hose on them that afternoon after kindergarten.

Howie was already following Henry across the street.

When Henry executed his sharp about-face on the opposite kerb, he saw that Ramona had been left behind. 'You were supposed to cross with me,' he told her. 'Now you have to wait until some more kids come.'

'I don't care,' said Ramona happily, and marched off to the muddy mud.

'Ramona, you come back here!' yelled Henry. 'You're going to get into trouble.'

'Traffic boys aren't supposed to talk on duty,' Ramona reminded him, and marched straight into the mud. Surprisingly her feet started to slide out from under her. She had not realized that mud was so slippery. Managing to regain her balance, she set each boot down slowly and carefully before she pulled her other boot from the sucking mud. She waved happily to Henry, who seemed to be going through some sort of struggle within himself. He kept opening his mouth, as if he wanted to say something, and then closing it again. Ramona also waved at the members of the morning kindergarten, who were watching her through the playground fence.

More mud clung to her boots with each step. 'Look at my elephant feet!' she called out. Her boots were becoming heavier and heavier.

Henry gave up his struggle. 'You're going to get stuck!' he yelled.

'No, I'm not!' insisted Ramona, and discovered she was unable to raise her right boot. She tried to raise her left boot, but it was stuck fast. She grasped the top of one of her boots with both hands and tried to lift her foot, but she could not budge it. She tried to lift the other foot, but she could not budge it either. Henry was right. Miss Binney was not going to like what had happened, but Ramona was stuck.

'I told you so!' yelled Henry against the traffic rules.

Ramona was becoming warmer and warmer inside her raincoat. She pulled and lifted. She could raise her feet, one at a time, inside her boots, but no matter how she tugged and yanked with her hands she could not lift her precious boots from the mud.

Ramona grew warmer and warmer. She could never get out of this mud. Kindergarten would start without her, and she would be left all alone in the mud. Miss Binney would not like her being out here in the mud, when she was supposed to be inside singing the dawnzer song and doing seat work. Ramona's chin began to quiver.

'Look at Ramona! Look at Ramona!' shrieked the kindergarten, as Miss Binney, in a raincoat and with a plastic hood over her hair, appeared on the playground.

'Oh dear!' Ramona heard Miss Binney say.

Drivers of cars paused to stare and smile as tears mingled with the rain on Ramona's cheeks. Miss Binney came splashing across the street. 'My goodness, Ramona, how are we going to get you out?'

'I d-don't know,' sobbed Ramona. Miss Binney could not get stuck in the mud, too. The morning kindergarten needed her.

A man called out from a car, 'What you need is a few boards.'

'Boards would only sink into the muck,' said a passer-by on the pavement.

The first bell rang. Ramona sobbed harder. Now Miss Binney would have to go into school and leave her out here alone in the mud and the rain and the cold. By now some of the older boys and girls were staring at her from the windows of the big school.

'Now don't worry, Ramona,' said Miss Binney. 'We'll get you out somehow.'

Ramona, who wanted to be helpful, knew what happened when a car was stuck in the mud. 'Could you call a t-tow t-truck?' she asked with a big sniff. She could see herself being yanked out of the mud by a heavy chain hooked on the collar of her raincoat. She found this picture so interesting that her sobs subsided, and she waited hopefully for Miss Binney's answer.

The second bell rang. Miss Binney was not looking at Ramona. She was looking thoughtfully at Henry Huggins, who seemed to be staring at something way off in the distance. The traffic sergeant blew his whistle summoning the traffic boys to return from their posts to school.

'Boy!' Miss Binney called out. 'Traffic boy!'

'Who? Me?' asked Henry, even though he was the only traffic boy stationed at that intersection.

'That's Henry Huggins,' said helpful Ramona.

'Henry, come here, please,' said Miss Binney.

'I'm supposed to go in when the whistle blows,' said Henry, as he glanced up at the boys and girls who were watching from the big brick building.

'But this is an emergency,' Miss Binney pointed out. 'You have boots on, and I need your help in getting this little girl out of the mud. I'll explain to the principal.'

Henry did not seem very enthusiastic as he splashed across the street, and when he came to the mud he heaved a big sigh before he stepped into it. Carefully he picked his way through the muck and the puddles to Ramona. 'Now see what you got me into,' he said crossly. 'I told you to keep out of here.'

For once Ramona had nothing to say. Henry was right.

'I guess I'll have to carry you,' he said, and his tone was grudging. 'Hang on.' He stooped and grasped Ramona around the waist, and she obediently put her arms around the wet collar of his raincoat. Henry was big and strong. Then, to Ramona's horror, she found herself being lifted right out of her beautiful new boots.

'My boots!' she wailed. 'You're leaving my boots!'

Henry slipped, slid, and in spite of Ramona's weight regained his balance. 'You keep quiet,' he ordered. 'I'm getting you out of here, aren't I? Do you want us both to land in the mud?'

Ramona hung on and said no more. Henry lurched and skidded through the mud to the pavement, where he set his burden down in front of Miss Binney.

'Yea!' yelled some big boys who had opened a window. 'Yea, Henry!' Henry scowled in their direction.

'Thank you, Henry,' said Miss Binney with real gratitude, as Henry tried to scrape the mud from his boots on the edge of the kerb. 'What do you say, Ramona?'

'My boots,' said Ramona. 'He left my new boots in the mud!' How lonely they looked, two bright spots of red in all that mud. She could not leave her boots behind, not when she had waited so long to get them. Somebody might take them, and she would have to go back to shoving her feet into Howie's ugly old boots.

'Don't worry, Ramona,' said Miss Binney, looking anxiously towards the rest of her morning kindergarten growing wetter by the minute as they watched through the fence. 'Nobody is going to take your boots on a day like this. We'll get them back when it stops raining and the ground dries off.'

'But they'll fill up with rain without my feet in them,' protested Ramona. 'The rain will spoil them.'

Miss Binney was sympathetic but firm. 'I know how you feel, but I'm afraid there isn't anything we can do about it.'

Miss Binney's words were too much for Ramona. After all the times she had been forced to wear Howie's ugly old brown boots she could not leave her beautiful new red boots out in the mud to fill up with rainwater. 'I want my boots,' she howled, and began to cry again.

'Oh, all right,' said Henry crossly. 'I'll get your old boots. Don't start crying again.' And heaving another gusty sigh, he waded back out into the empty lot, yanked the boots out of the mud, and waded back to the pavement, where he dropped them at Ramona's feet. 'There,' he said, looking at the mud-covered objects with dislike.

Ramona expected him to add, I hope you're satisfied, but he did not. He just started across the street to school.

'Thank you, Henry,' Ramona called after him without being reminded. There was something very special about being rescued by a big, strong traffic boy in a yellow raincoat.

Miss Binney picked up the muddy boots, and said, 'What beautiful red boots. We'll wash off the mud in the sink, and they'll be as good as new. And now we must hurry back to the kindergarten.'

Ramona smiled at Miss Binney, who was again, she decided, the nicest, most understanding teacher in the world. Not once had Miss Binney scolded or made any tiresome remarks about why on earth did Ramona have to do such a thing. Not once had Miss Binney said she should know better.

Then something on the pavement caught Ramona's eye. It was a pink worm that still had some wiggle left in it. She picked it up and wound it around her finger as she looked towards Henry. 'I'm going to marry you, Henry Huggins!' she called out.

Even though traffic boys were supposed to stand up straight, Henry seemed to hunch down inside his raincoat as if he were trying to disappear.

'I've got an engagement ring, and I'm going to marry you!' yelled Ramona after Henry, as the morning kindergarten laughed and cheered.

'Yea, Henry!' yelled the big boys, before their teacher shut the window.

As she followed Miss Binney across the street Ramona heard Davy's joyful shout. 'Boy, I'm glad it isn't me!'

Chapter 6
The Baddest Witch in the World

When the morning kindergarten cut jack-o'-lan-
terns from orange paper and pasted them on the
windows so that the light shone through the eye
and mouth holes, Ramona knew that at last Hallowe'en was not far away. Next to Christmas and
her birthday, Ramona liked Hallowe'en best. She
liked dressing up and going trick-or-treating after
dark with Beezus. She liked those nights when the

bare branches of trees waved against the street-lights, and the world was a ghostly place. Ramona liked scaring people, and she liked the shivery feeling of being scared herself.

Ramona had always enjoyed going to school with her mother to watch the boys and girls of Glenwood School parade on the playground in their Halloween costumes. Afterwards she used to eat a doughnut and drink a paper cup of apple juice if there happened to be some left over. This year, after years of sitting on the benches with mothers and little brothers and sisters, Ramona was finally going to get to wear a costume and march around and around the playground. This year she had a doughnut and apple juice coming to her.

'Mama, did you buy my mask?' Ramona asked every day, when she came home from school.

'Not today, dear,' Mrs Quimby answered. 'Don't pester. I'll get it the next time I go down to the shopping centre.'

Ramona, who did not mean to pester her mother, could not see why grown-ups had to be so slow. 'Make it a bad mask, Mama,' she said. 'I want to be the baddest witch in the whole world.'

'You mean the worst witch,' Beezus said, whenever she happened to overhear this conversation.

'I do not,' contradicted Ramona. 'I mean the

baddest witch.' 'Baddest witch' sounded much scarier than 'worst witch', and Ramona did enjoy stories about bad witches, the badder the better. She had no patience with books about good witches, because witches were supposed to be bad. Ramona had chosen to be a witch for that very reason.

Then one day when Ramona came home from school she found two paper bags on the foot of her bed. One contained black material and a pattern for a witch costume. The picture on the pattern showed the witch's hat pointed like the letter A. Ramona reached into the second bag and pulled out a rubber witch mask so scary that she quickly dropped it on the bed because she was not sure she even wanted to touch it. The flabby thing was the greyish-green colour of mould and had stringy hair, a hooked nose, snaggle teeth, and a wart on its nose. Its empty eyes seemed to stare at Ramona with a look of evil. The face was so ghastly that Ramona had to remind herself that it was only a rubber mask from the toy store before she could summon enough courage to pick it up and slip it over her head.

Ramona peeked cautiously in the mirror, backed away, and then gathered her courage for a longer look. That's really me in there, she told herself and felt better. She ran off to show her mother and discovered that she felt very brave when she was inside the mask and did not have to look at it. 'I'm the baddest witch in the world!' she shouted, her voice muffled by the mask, and was delighted when her mother was so frightened she dropped her sewing.

Ramona waited for Beezus and her father to come home, so she could put on her mask and jump out and scare them. But that night, before she went to bed, she rolled up the mask and hid it behind a cushion of the couch in the living-room.

'What are you doing that for?' asked Beezus, who had nothing to be afraid of. She was planning to be a princess and wear a narrow pink mask.

'Because I want to,' answered Ramona, who did

not care to sleep in the same room with that ghastly, leering face.

Afterwards when Ramona wanted to frighten herself she would lift the cushion for a quick glimpse of her scary mask before she clapped the pillow over it again. Scaring herself was such fun.

When Ramona's costume was finished and the day of the Hallowe'en parade arrived, the morning kindergarten had trouble sitting still for seat work. They wiggled so much while resting on their mats that Miss Binney had to wait a long time before she found someone quiet enough to be the wake-up fairy. When kindergarten was finally dismissed, the whole class forgot the rules and went stampeding out the door. At home Ramona ate only the soft part of her tuna-fish sandwich, because her mother insisted she could not go to the Hallowe'en parade on an empty stomach. She wadded the crusts into her paper napkin and hid them beneath the edge of her plate before she ran to her room to put on her long black dress, her cape, her mask, and her pointed witch hat held on by an elastic under her chin. Ramona had doubts about that elastic – none of the witches whom she met in books seemed to have elastic under their chin – but today she was too happy and excited to bother to make a fuss.

'See, Mama!' she cried. 'I'm the baddest witch in the world!'

Mrs Quimby smiled at Ramona, patted her through the long black dress, and said affectionately, 'Sometimes I think you are.'

'Come on, Mama! Let's go to the Hallowe'en parade.' Ramona had waited so long that she did not see how she could wait another five minutes.

'I told Howie's mother we would wait for them,' said Mrs Quimby.

'Mama, did you have to?' protested Ramona, running to the front window to watch for Howie. Fortunately, Mrs Kemp and Willa Jean were already approaching with Howie dressed in a black cat costume lagging along behind holding the end of his tail in one hand. Willa Jean in her stroller was wearing a buck-toothed rabbit mask.

Ramona could not wait. She burst out the front door yelling through her mask, 'Yah! Yah! I'm the baddest witch in the world! Hurry, Howie! I'm going to get you, Howie!'

Howie walked stolidly along, lugging his tail, so Ramona ran out to meet him. He was not wearing a mask, but instead had pipe cleaners Scotch-taped to his face for whiskers.

'I'm the baddest witch in the world,' Ramona informed him, 'And you can be my cat.'

'I don't want to be your cat,' said Howie. 'I don't want to be a cat at all.'

'Why not, Howie?' asked Mrs Quimby, who had joined Ramona and the Kemps. 'I think you make a very nice cat.'

'My tail is busted,' complained Howie. 'I don't want to be a cat with a busted tail.'

Mrs Kemp sighed. 'Now Howie, if you'll just hold up the end of your tail nobody will notice.' Then she said to Mrs Quimby, 'I promised him a pirate costume, but his older sister was sick and while I was taking her temperature Willa Jean crawled into a cupboard and managed to dump a whole quart of salad oil all over the kitchen floor. If you've ever had to clean oil off a floor, you know what I went through, and then Howie went into the bathroom and climbed up – yes, dear, I understand you wanted to help – to get a sponge, and he accidentally knelt on a tube of toothpaste that someone had left the top off of – now Howie, I didn't say you left the top off – and toothpaste squirted all over the bathroom, and there was another mess to clean up. Well, I finally had to drag his sister's old cat costume out of a drawer, and when he put it on we discovered the wire in the tail was broken, but there wasn't time to rip it apart and put in a new wire.'

'You have a handsome set of whiskers,' said Mrs Quimby, trying to coax Howie to look on the bright side.

'Scotch tape itches me,' said Howie.

Ramona could see that Howie was not going to be any fun at all, even on Hallowe'en. Never mind. She would have fun all by herself. 'I'm the baddest witch in the world,' she sang in her muffled voice, skipping with both feet. 'I'm the baddest witch in the world.'

When they were in sight of the playground, Ramona saw that it was already swarming with both the morning and the afternoon kindergartens in their Hallowe'en costumes. Poor Miss Binney, dressed like Mother Goose, now had the responsibility of sixty-eight boys and girls. 'Run along, Ramona,' said Mrs Quimby, when they had crossed the street. 'Howie's mother and I will go around to the big playground and try to find a seat on a bench before they are all taken.'

Ramona ran screaming on to the playground. 'Yah! Yah! I'm the baddest witch in the world!' Nobody paid any attention, because everyone else was screaming, too. The noise was glorious. Ramona yelled and screamed and shrieked and chased anyone who would run. She chased tramps and ghosts and ballerinas. Sometimes other witches in masks exactly like hers chased her, and then she would turn around and chase the witches right back. She tried to chase Howie, but he would not run. He just stood beside the fence holding his broken tail and missing all the fun.

Ramona discovered dear little Davy in a skimpy pirate costume from the toy store. She could tell he was Davy by his thin legs. At last! She pounced and kissed him through her rubber mask. Davy looked startled, but he had the presence of mind to make a gagging noise while Ramona raced away, satisfied that she finally had managed to catch and kiss Davy.

Then Ramona saw Susan getting out of her mother's car. As she might have guessed, Susan was

dressed as an old-fashioned girl with a long skirt, an apron, and pantalettes. 'I'm the baddest witch in the world!' yelled Ramona, and ran after Susan whose curls bobbed daintily about her shoulders in a way that could not be disguised. Ramona was unable to resist. After weeks of longing she tweaked one of Susan's curls, and yelled, *'Boing!'* through her rubber mask.

'You stop that,' said Susan, and smoothed her curls.

'Yah! Yah! I'm the baddest witch in the world!' Ramona was carried away. She tweaked another curl and yelled a muffled *'Boing!'*

A clown laughed and joined Ramona. He too tweaked a curl and yelled, *'Boing!'*

The old-fashioned girl stamped her foot. 'You stop that!' she said angrily.

'Boing! Boing!' Others joined the game. Susan tried to run away, but no matter which way she ran there was someone eager to stretch a curl and yell, *'Boing!'* Susan ran to Miss Binny. 'Miss Binney! Miss Binney!' she cried. 'They're teasing me! They're pulling my hair and boinging me!'

'Who's teasing you?' asked Miss Binney.

'Everybody,' said Susan tearfully. 'A witch started it.'

'Which witch?' asked Miss Binney.

Susan looked around. 'I don't know which witch,' she said, 'but it was a bad witch.'

That's me, the baddest witch in the world, thought Ramona. At the same time she was a little surprised. That others really would not know that she was behind her mask had never occurred to her.

'Never mind, Susan,' said Miss Binny. 'You stay near me, and no one will tease you.'

Which witch, thought Ramona, liking the sound of the words. Which witch, which witch. As the words ran through her thoughts Ramona began to wonder if Miss Binney could guess who she was. She ran up to her teacher and shouted in her muffled voice, 'Hello, Miss Binney! I'm going to get you, Miss Binney!'

'Ooh, what a scary witch!' said Miss Binney, rather absentmindedly, Ramona thought. Plainly Miss Binney was not really frightened, and with so many witches running around she had not recognized Ramona.

No, Miss Binney was not the one who was frightened. Ramona was. Miss Binney did not know who this witch was. Nobody knew who Ramona was, and if nobody knew who she was, she wasn't anybody.

'Get out of the way, old witch!' Eric R. yelled at

Ramona. He did not say, Get out of the way, Ramona.

Ramona could not remember a time when there was not someone near who knew who she was. Even last Hallowe'en, when she dressed up as a ghost and went trick-or-treating with Beezus and the older boys and girls, everyone seemed to know who she was. 'I can guess who this little ghost is,' the neighbours said, as they dropped a miniature candy bar or a handful of peanuts into her paper bag. And now, with so many witches running around and still more witches on the big playground, no one knew who she was.

'Davy, guess who I am!' yelled Ramona. Surely Davy would know.

'You're just another old witch,' answered Davy.

The feeling was the scariest one Ramona had ever experienced. She felt lost inside her costume. She wondered if her mother would know which witch was which, and the thought that her own mother might not know her frightened Ramona even more. What if her mother forgot her? What if everyone in the whole world forgot her? With that terrifying thought Ramona snatched off her mask, and although its ugliness was no longer the most frightening thing about it, she rolled it up so she would not have to look at it.

How cool the air felt outside that dreadful mask! Ramona no longer wanted to be the baddest witch in the world. She wanted to be Ramona Geraldine Quimby and be sure that Miss Binney and everyone on the playground knew her. Around her the ghosts and tramps and pirates raced and shouted, but Ramona stood near the door of the kindergarten quietly watching.

Davy raced up to her and yelled. 'Yah! You can't catch me!'

'I don't want to catch you,' Ramona informed him.

Davy looked surprised and a little disappointed, but he ran off on his thin little legs, shouting, 'Yo-ho-ho and a bottle of rum!'

Joey yelled after him, 'You're not really a pirate. You're just Mush Pot Davy!'

Miss Binney was trying to herd her sixty-eight charges into a double line. Two mothers who felt sorry for the teacher were helping round up the kindergarten to start the Hallowe'en parade, but as always there were some children who would rather run around than do what they were supposed to do.

For once Ramona was not one of them. On the big playground someone started to play a marching record through a loudspeaker. The Hallowe'en parade that Ramona had looked forward to since she was in nursery school was about to begin.

'Come along, children,' said Miss Binney. Seeing Ramona standing alone, she said, 'Come on, Ramona.'

It was a great relief to Ramona to hear Miss Binney speak her name, to hear her teacher say 'Ramona' when she was looking at her. But as much as Ramona longed to prance along to the marching music with the rest of her class, she did not move to join them.

'Put on your mask, Ramona, and get in line,' said Miss Binney, guiding a ghost and a gypsy into place.

Ramona wanted to obey her teacher, but at the same time she was afraid of losing herself behind that scary mask. The line of kindergarteners, all of them wearing masks except Howie with his pipe-cleaner whiskers, was less straggly now, and everyone was eager to start the parade. If Ramona did not do something quickly she would be left behind, and she could not let such a thing happen, not when she had waited so many years to be in a Hallowe'en parade.

Ramona took only a moment to decide what to do. She ran to her cupboard inside the kindergarten building and snatched a crayon from her box. Then she grabbed a piece of paper from the supply cupboard. Outside she could hear the many feet of the morning and afternoon kindergartens marching off to the big playground. There was no time for Ramona's best printing, but that was all right. This job was not seat work to be supervised by Miss Binney. As fast as she could Ramona printed her name, and then she could not resist adding with a

flourish her last initial complete with ears and whiskers.

RAMONA 🐱

Now the whole world would know who she was! She was Ramona Quimby, the only girl in the world with ears and whiskers on her last initial. Ramona pulled on her rubber mask, clapped her pointed hat on top of it, snapped the elastic under her chin, and ran after her class as it marched on to the big playground. She did not care if she was last in line and had to march beside gloomy old Howie still lugging his broken tail.

Around the playground marched the kindergarten followed by the first grade and all the other grades while mothers and little brothers and sisters watched. Ramona felt very grown-up remembering how last year she had been a little sister sitting on a bench watching for her big sister Beezus to march by and hoping for a left-over doughnut.

'Yah! Yah! I'm the baddest witch in the world!' Ramona chanted, as she held up her sign for all to see. Around the playground she marched towards her mother, who was waiting on the bench. Her mother saw her, pointed her out to Mrs Kemp, and waved. Ramona beamed inside her stuffy mask. Her mother recognized her!

Poor little Willa Jean in her stroller could not read, so Ramona called out to her, 'It's me, Willa Jean. I'm Ramona, the baddest witch in the world!'

Willa Jean in her rabbit mask understood. She laughed and slapped her hands on the tray of her stroller.

Ramona saw Henry's dog Ribsy trotting along, supervising the parade. 'Yah! Ribsy! I'm going to get you, Ribsy!' she threatened, as she marched past.

Ribsy gave a short bark, and Ramona was sure that even Ribsy knew who she was as she marched off to collect her doughnut and apple juice.

Chapter 7
The Day Things Went Wrong

Ramona's day was off to a promising start for two reasons, both of which proved she was growing up. First of all, she had a loose tooth, a very loose tooth, a tooth that waggled back and forth with only a little help from her tongue. It was probably the loosest tooth in the morning kindergarten, which meant that the tooth fairy would finally pay a visit to Ramona before long.

Ramona had her suspicions about the tooth fairy. She had seen Beezus search under her pillow in the morning, after losing a tooth, and then call out, 'Daddy, my tooth is still here. The tooth fairy forgot to come!'

'That's funny,' Mr Quimby would answer. 'Are you sure?'

'Positive. I looked everyplace for the money.'

'Let me look,' was always Mr Quimby's suggestion. Somehow he could always find the tooth fairy's coin when Beezus could not.

Now Ramona's turn would soon come. She planned to stay awake and trap the tooth fairy to make sure it really was her father.

Not only did Ramona have a loose tooth to make her feel that she was finally beginning to grow up, she was going to get to walk to school all by herself. At last! Howie was home with a cold, and her mother had to drive Beezus downtown for an early dental appointment.

'Now Ramona,' said Mrs Quimby, as she put on her coat, 'I'm going to trust you to stay all by yourself for a little while before you start to school. Do you think you can be a good girl?'

'Of course, Mama,' said Ramona, who felt that she was always a good girl.

'Now be sure you watch the clock,' said Mrs Quimby, 'and leave for school at exactly quarter past eight.'

'Yes, Mama.'

'And look both ways before you cross the street.'

'Yes, Mama.'

Mrs Quimby kissed Ramona good-bye. 'And be sure to close the door behind you when you leave.'

'Yes, Mama,' was Ramona's tolerant answer. She could not see why her mother was anxious.

When Mrs Quimby and Beezus had gone, Ramona sat down at the kitchen table to wiggle her tooth and watch the clock. The little hand was at eight, and the big hand was at one. Ramona wiggled her tooth with her finger. Then she wiggled it with her tongue, back and forth, back and forth. The big hand crept to two. Ramona took hold of her tooth with her fingers, but as much as she longed to surprise her mother with an empty space in her mouth, actually pulling the tooth was too scary. She went back to wiggling.

The big hand moved slowly to three. Ramona continued to sit on the chair wiggling her tooth and being a very good girl as she had promised. The big hand crawled along to four. When it reached five, Ramona knew that it would be quarter past eight and time to go to school. A quarter was twenty-five cents. Therefore, a quarter past eight was twenty-five minutes after eight. She had figured the answer out all by herself.

At last the big hand crawled to five. Ramona slid off the chair and slammed the door behind her as she started off to school alone. So far, so good, but as soon as Ramona reached the pavement, she realized that something was wrong. In a moment she understood what it was. The street was too quiet. No one else was walking to school. Ramona stopped in confusion. Maybe she was mixed up. Maybe today was really Saturday. Maybe her mother forgot to look at the calendar.

No, it could not be Saturday because yesterday was Sunday. Besides, there was Henry Huggins's dog Ribsy, trotting along the street on his way home from escorting Henry to school. Today really was a school day, because Ribsy followed Henry to school every morning. Maybe the clock was wrong. In a panic Ramona began to run. Miss Binney would not want her to be late for school. She did manage to slow down and look both ways before she walked across the streets, but when she saw that Henry was not guarding his usual intersection, she knew that the traffic boys had gone in and she was even later than she had thought. She ran across the kindergarten playground, and then stopped. The door of the kindergarten was shut. Miss Binney had started school without her.

Ramona stood puffing a moment trying to catch her breath. Of course, she could not expect Miss Binney to wait for her when she was late, but she could not help wishing that her teacher had missed her so much she had said, 'Class, let's wait for Ramona. Kindergarten isn't any fun without Ramona.'

When Ramona caught her breath, she knew what she should do. She knocked and waited for the door monitor to open the door. The monitor turned out to be Susan, who said accusingly, 'You're late.'

'Never mind, Susan,' said Miss Binney, who was standing in front of the class holding up a brown paper sack with a big *T* printed on it. 'What happened, Ramona?'

'I don't know,' Ramona was forced to admit. 'I left at a quarter past eight like my mother told me.'

Miss Binney smiled, and said, 'Next time try to walk a little faster,' before she continued where she had left off. 'Now who can guess what I have in this bag with the letter *T* printed on it? Remember, it is something that begins with *T*. Who can tell me how *T* sounds?'

'T-t-t-t-t,' ticked the kindergarten.

'Good,' said Miss Binney. 'Davy, what do you think is in the *b*ag?' Miss Binney was inclined to bear down on the first letters of words now that the class was working on the sounds letters make.

'Taterpillars?' said Davy hopefully. He rarely got anything right, but he kept trying.

'No, Davy. *C*aterpillar begins with *C*. C-c-c-c-c. What I have in the *b*ag begins with *T*. T-t-t-t-t.'

Davy was crestfallen. He had been so sure caterpillar began with *T*.

T-t-t-t-t. The class ticked quietly while it thought. 'T. V.?' someone suggested. T. V. began with *T*, but was not in the bag.

'T-t-t-t-t-tadpoles?' Wrong.

'Teeter-totter?' Wrong again. How could anyone have a teeter-totter in a paper bag?

T-t-t-t-t, Ramona ticked to herself as she wiggled her tooth with her fingers. 'Tooth?' she suggested.

'*T*ooth is a good *T* word, Ramona,' said Miss Binney, 'but it is not what I have in the *b*ag.'

Ramona was so pleased by Miss Binney's compliment that she wiggled her tooth even harder and suddenly found it in her hand. A strange taste filled her mouth. Ramona stared at her little tooth and was astonished to discover that one end was

bloody. 'Miss Binney!' she cried without raising her hand. 'My tooth came out!'

Someone had lost a tooth! The kindergarten began to crowd around Ramona. 'Seats, please, boys and girls,' said Miss Binney. 'Ramona, you may go rinse your mouth, and then you may show us your *t*ooth.'

Ramona did as she was told, and when she held up her tooth for all to admire, Miss Binney said, '*T*ooth. T-t-t-t-t.' When Ramona pulled down her lip to show the hole where her tooth had been, Miss Binney did not say anything because the class was working on *T* and hole did not begin with *T*. It turned out that Miss Binney had a t-t-t-t-tiger, stuffed, of course, in the *b*ag.

Before the class started seat work, Ramona went to her teacher with her precious bloody tooth, and asked, 'Would you keep this for me?' Ramona wanted to be sure she did not lose her tooth, because she needed it for bait to catch the tooth fairy. She planned to pile a lot of clattery things like saucepans and pie tins and old broken toys beside her bed so the tooth fairy would trip and wake her up.

Miss Binney smiled as she opened a drawer of her desk. 'Your first *t*ooth! Of course, I'll keep it safe so you can take it home for the *t*ooth *f*airy. You're a brave girl.'

Ramona loved Miss Binney for understanding. She loved Miss Binney for not being cross when she was late for school. She loved Miss Binney for telling her she was a brave girl.

Ramona was so happy that the morning went quickly. Seat work was unusually interesting. The kindergarten now had sheets of pictures, three to a row, printed in purple ink by a copy machine. One row showed a top, a girl and a toe. The kindergarten was supposed to circle the top and the toe, because they both began with *T*, and cross out the girl, because girl began with a different sound.

Ramona dearly loved to circle and cross out, and was sorry when recess time came.

'Want to see where my tooth was?' Ramona asked Eric J., when the class had finished with *T* for the day and had gone out to the playground. She opened her mouth and pulled down her lower lip.

Eric J. was filled with admiration. 'Where your tooth was is all bloody,' he told her.

The glory of losing a tooth! Ramona ran over to Susan. 'Want to see where my tooth was?' she asked.

'No,' said Susan, 'and I'm glad you were late, because I got to open the door my very first day as door monitor.'

Ramona was indignant that Susan had refused to admire the bloody hole in her mouth. No one else bravely had lost a tooth during kindergarten. Ramona seized one of Susan's curls, and, careful not to pull hard enough to hurt Susan, she stretched it out and let it spring back. *'Boing!'* she cried and ran off, circling the jungle gym and coming back to Susan, who was about to climb the steps to the travelling bars. She stretched another curl and yelled, *'Boing!'*

'Ramona Quimby!' shrieked Susan. 'You stop boinging me!'

Ramona was filled with the glory of losing her

first tooth and love for her teacher. Miss Binney had said she was brave! This day was the most wonderful day in the world! The sun shone, the sky was blue, and Miss Binney loved her. Ramona flung out her arms and circled the jungle gym once more on feet light with joy. She swooped towards Susan, stretched a curl, and uttered a long-drawn-out '*Boi-i-ing!*'

'Miss Binney!' cried Susan on the verge of tears. 'Ramona is boinging me, and I bet she was

the witch who boinged me at the Hallowe'en parade!'

Tattletale, thought Ramona scornfully, as she circled the jungle gym on feet of joy. Circle Ramona, cross out Susan!

'Ramona,' said Miss Binney, as Ramona flew past. 'Come here. I want to talk to you.'

Ramona turned back and looked expectantly at her teacher.

'Ramona, you must stop pulling Susan's hair,' said Miss Binney.

'Yes, Miss Binney,' said Ramona, and skipped off to the travelling bars.

Ramona intended to stop pulling Susan's curls, she truly did, but unfortunately Susan would not cooperate. When recess was over and the class was filing back into the room, Susan turned to Ramona, and said, 'You're a big pest.'

Susan could not have chosen a word that Ramona would resent more. Beezus was always saying she was a pest. The big boys and girls on Ramona's street called her a pest, but Ramona did not consider herself a pest. People who called her a pest did not understand that a littler person sometimes had to be a little bit noisier and a little bit more stubborn in order to be noticed at all. Ramona had to put up with being called a pest by older boys and girls, but she did not have to put up with being called a pest by a girl her own age.

'I'm not a pest,' said Ramona indignantly, and to get even she stretched one of Susan's curls and whispered, *'Boing!'*

Ramona's luck was bad, however, for Miss Binney happened to be watching. 'Come here, Ramona,' said her teacher.

Ramona had a terrible feeling that this time Miss Binney was not going to understand.

'Ramona, I'm disappointed in you.' Miss Binney's voice was serious.

Ramona had never seen her teacher look so serious. 'Susan called me a pest,' she said in a small voice.

'That is no excuse for pulling hair,' said Miss Binney. 'I told you to stop pulling Susan's hair, and I meant it. If you cannot stop pulling Susan's hair, you will have to go home and stay there until you can.'

Ramona was shocked. Miss Binney did not love her anymore. The class was suddenly quiet, and Ramona could almost feel their stares against her back as she stood there looking at the floor.

'Do you think you can stop pulling Susan's hair?' asked Miss Binney.

Ramona thought. Could she really stop pulling Susan's curls? She thought about those thick, springy locks that were so tempting. She thought about Susan, who always acted big. In kindergarten there was no worse crime than acting big. In the eyes of the children acting big was worse than being

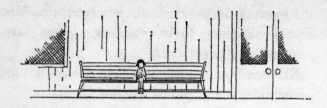

a pest. Ramona finally looked up at Miss Binney and gave her an honest answer. 'No,' she said. 'I can't.'

Miss Binney looked a little surprised. 'Very well, Ramona. You will have to go home and stay there until you can make up your mind not to pull Susan's curls.'

'Now?' asked Ramona in a small voice.

'You may sit outside on the bench until it's time to go home,' said Miss Binney. 'I'm sorry, Ramona, but we cannot have a hair puller in our kindergarten.'

No one said a word as Ramona turned and walked out of the kindergarten and sat down on the bench. The little children next door stared at her through the fence. The workmen across the street looked at her in amusement. Ramona gave a long shuddering sigh, but she just managed to hold back the tears. Nobody was going to see Ramona Quimby acting like a baby.

'That girl has been bad again,' Ramona heard

Chapter 8
Kindergarten Dropout

'Why, Ramona, whatever is the matter?' Mrs Quimby wanted to know, when Ramona opened the back door.

'Oh . . . nothing.' Ramona had no trouble hiding the gap in her teeth. She did not feel like smiling, and not having a tooth to leave for the tooth fairy was only a small part of her trouble.

Mrs Quimby laid her hand on Ramona's forehead. 'Are you feeling all right?' she asked.

the four-year-old next door say to her little sister.

When the bell rang, Miss Binney opened the door to see her class out, and said to Ramona, 'I hope you'll decide you can stop pulling Susan's hair so you can come back to kindergarten.'

Ramona did not answer. Her feet, no longer light with joy, carried her slowly towards home. She could never go to kindergarten, because Miss Binney did not love her anymore. She would never get to show-and-tell or play Grey Duck again. She wouldn't get to work on the paper turkey Miss Binney was going to teach the class to make for Thanksgiving. Ramona sniffed and wiped the sleeve of her sweater across her eyes. She did love kindergarten, but it was all over now. Cross out Ramona.

Not until she was half-way home did Ramona remember her precious tooth in Miss Binney's desk.

'Yes, I feel all right,' answered Ramona, meaning that she did not have a broken leg, a skinned knee, or a sore throat.

'Then something must be wrong,' insisted Mrs Quimby. 'I can tell by your face.'

Ramona sighed. 'Miss Binney doesn't like me any more,' she confessed.

'Of course Miss Binney likes you,' said Mrs Quimby. 'She may not like some of the things you do, but she likes you.'

'No, she doesn't,' contradicted Ramona. 'She doesn't want me there any more.' Ramona felt sad thinking about the recesses and the new seat work she was going to miss.

'Why, what do you mean?' Mrs Quimby was puzzled. 'Of course Miss Binney wants you there.'

'No, she doesn't,' insisted Ramona. 'She told me not to come back.'

'But why?'

'She doesn't like me,' was Ramona's answer.

Mrs Quimby was exasperated. 'Then something must have happened. There is only one thing to do, and that is to go to school and find out. Eat your lunch, and we'll go to school before afternoon kindergarten starts and see what this is all about.'

After Ramona had picked at her sandwich

awhile, Mrs Quimby said briskly, 'Put on your sweater, Ramona, and come along.'

'No,' said Ramona. 'I'm not going.'

'Oh yes, you are, young lady,' said her mother, and took her daughter by the hand.

Ramona knew she had no choice when her mother started calling her young lady. She dragged her feet as much as she could on the way to school, where the afternoon kindergarten was behaving like the morning kindergarten. Half the class was lined up by the door waiting for Miss Binney while the other half raced around the playground. Ramona stared at the ground, because she did not want anyone to see her, and when Miss Binney arrived, Mrs Quimby asked to talk to her for a moment.

Ramona did not look up. Her mother led her to the bench beside the kindergarten door. 'You sit there and don't budge while I have a little talk with Miss Binney,' she told Ramona.

Ramona sat on the bench swinging her feet, thinking about her tooth in Miss Binney's drawer and wondering what her teacher and her mother were saying about her. Finally she could stand the suspense no longer. She had to budge so she slipped over to the door, as close as she could without being seen, and listened. The afternoon kindergarten and the workmen across the street were making so much noise she could catch only a few phrases such as 'bright and imaginative,' 'ability to get along with her peer group,' and 'negative desire for attention.' Ramona felt awed and frightened to be discussed in such strange big words, which must mean Miss Binney thought she was very bad indeed. She scuttled back to the bench when at last she heard her mother walk to the door.

'What did she say?' Ramona's curiosity was almost more than she could endure.

Mrs Quimby looked stern. 'She said she will be glad to have you back when you are ready to come back.'

'Then I'm not going back,' announced Ramona. She would never go to kindergarten at all if her teacher did not like her. Never.

'Oh yes, you are,' said Mrs Quimby wearily.

Ramona knew better.

Thus began a difficult time in the Quimby household. 'But Ramona, you have to go to kindergarten,' protested Beezus, when she came home from school that afternoon. 'Everybody goes to kindergarten.'

'I don't,' said Ramona. 'I used to, but I don't now.'

When Mr Quimby came home from work, Mrs

Quimby took him aside and talked quietly to him. Ramona was not fooled for a minute. She knew exactly what those whispers were about.

'Well, Ramona, suppose you tell me all about what went on at school today,' said Mr Quimby with that false cheerfulness grown-ups use when they are trying to persuade children to tell something they don't want to tell.

Ramona, who longed to run to her father and show him where her tooth used to be, thought awhile before she said, 'We guessed what Miss Binney had in a paper bag that began with a *T*, and Davy guessed 'taterpillars.''

'And what else happened?' asked Mr Quimby, all set to be patient.

Ramona could not tell her father about her tooth, and she was not going to tell about pulling Susan's curls. Nothing much was left to talk about. 'We learned *T*,' she said at last.

Mr Quimby gave his daughter a long look, but said nothing.

After dinner Beezus talked to Mary Jane on the telephone, and Ramona heard her say, 'Guess what! Ramona is a kindergarten dropout!' She seemed to think this remark was very funny, because she giggled into the telephone. Ramona was not amused.

Later Beezus settled down to read a book while Ramona got out her crayons and some paper.

'Beezus, you don't have a very good light for reading,' said Mrs Quimby. And she added as she always did, 'You have only one pair of eyes, you know.'

Here was an opportunity for Ramona to show off her new kindergarten knowledge. 'Why don't you turn on the dawnzer?' she asked, proud of her new word.

Beezus looked up from her book. 'What are you talking about?' she asked Ramona. 'What's a dawnzer?'

Ramona was scornful. 'Silly. Everybody knows what a dawnzer is.'

'I don't,' said Mr Quimby, who had been reading the evening paper. 'What is a dawnzer?'

'A lamp,' said Ramona. 'It gives a lee light. We sing about it every morning in kindergarten.'

A puzzled silence fell over the room until Beezus suddenly shouted with laughter. 'She-she means – ' she gasped, *'The Star-Spangled B-banner!'* Her laughter dwindled to giggles. 'She means the *dawn's early light*.' She pronounced each word with exaggerated distinctness, and then she began to laugh again.

Ramona looked at her mother and father, who

had the straight mouths and laughing eyes of grown-ups who were trying not to laugh out loud. Beezus was right and she was wrong. She was nothing but a girl who used to go to kindergarten and who got everything wrong and made everyone laugh. She was a stupid little sister. A dumb stupid little sister, who never did anything right.

Suddenly everything that had happened that day was too much for Ramona. She glared at her sister, made a big crisscross motion in the air with her hand, and shouted, 'Cross out Beezus!' Then she threw her crayons on the floor, stamped her feet, burst into tears, and ran into the room she shared with her sister.

'Ramona Quimby!' her father said sternly, and Ramona knew that she was about to be ordered back to pick up her crayons. Well, her father could order all he wanted to. She was not going to pick up her crayons. Nobody could make her pick up her crayons. Nobody. Not her father nor her mother. Not even the principal. Not even God.

'Now, never mind,' Ramona heard her mother say. 'Poor little girl. She's upset. She's had a difficult day.'

Sympathy made things worse. 'I am *not* upset!' yelled Ramona, and yelling made her feel so much better that she continued. 'I am *not* upset, and I'm

not a *little* girl, and everybody is *mean* to laugh at me!' She threw herself on her bed and pounded her heels on the bedspread, but pounding on the bedclothes was not bad enough. Far from it.

Ramona wanted to be wicked, really wicked, so she swung around and beat her heels on the wall. Bang! Bang! Bang! That noise ought to make everybody good and mad. 'Mean, mean, mean!' she yelled, in time to her drumming heels. She wanted to make her whole family feel as angry as she felt. 'Mean, mean, mean!' She was glad her heels left marks on the wallpaper. Glad! Glad! Glad!

'Mother, Ramona's kicking the wall,' cried tat-

tletale Beezus, as if her mother did not know what Ramona was doing. 'It's my wall, too!'

Ramona did not care if Beezus tattled. She wanted her to tattle. Ramona wanted the whole world to know she was so bad she kicked the wall and left heel marks on the wallpaper.

'Ramona, if you're going to do that you had better take off your shoes.' Mrs Quimby's voice from the living room was tired but calm.

Ramona drummed harder to show everyone how bad she was. She would *not* take off her shoes. She was a terrible, wicked girl! Being such a bad, terrible, horrid, wicked girl made her feel *good*! She brought both heels against the wall at the same time. Thump! Thump! Thump! She was not the least bit sorry for what she was doing. She would *never* be sorry. Never! Never! Never!

'Ramona!' Mr Quimby's voice held a warning note. 'Do you want me to come in there?'

Ramona paused and considered. Did she want her father to come in? No, she did not. Her father, her mother, nobody could understand how hard it was to be a little sister. She drummed her heels a few more times to prove that her spirit was not broken. Then she lay on her bed and thought wild fierce thoughts until her mother came and silently helped her undress and get into bed. When the light had been turned out, Ramona felt so limp and tired that she soon fell asleep. After all she had no reason to try to stay awake, because the tooth fairy was not going to come to her house that night.

The next morning Mrs Quimby walked into the girls' room, and said briskly to Ramona, 'Which dress do you want to wear to school today?'

The empty space in her mouth and the heel marks on the wall above her bed reminded Ramona of all that had happened the day before. 'I'm not going to school,' she said, and reached for her play-clothes while Beezus put on a fresh school dress.

A terrible day had begun. No one said much at breakfast. Howie, who had recovered from his cold, stopped for Ramona on his way to school, and then went on without her. Ramona watched all the children in the neighbourhood go to school, and when the street was quiet, she turned on the television set.

Her mother turned it off, saying, 'Little girls who don't go to school can't watch television.'

Ramona felt that her mother did not understand. She wanted to go to school. She wanted to go to school more than anything in the world, but she could not go back when her teacher did not like her. Ramona got out her crayons and paper, which someone had put away for her, and settled down to draw. She drew a bird, a cat, and a ball in a row, and then with her red crayon she crossed out the cat, because it did not begin with the same sound as bird and ball. Afterwards she covered a whole sheet of paper with *Q*'s, Ramona-style, with ears and whiskers.

Ramona's mother did not feel sorry for Ramona. She merely said, 'Get your sweater, Ramona. I have to drive down to the shopping centre.' Ramona wished she had money from the tooth fairy to spend.

There followed the most boring morning of Ramona's entire life. She trailed along after her mother in the shopping centre while Mrs Quimby bought socks for Beezus, some buttons and thread, pillowcases that were on sale, a new electric cord for the waffle iron, a package of paper for Ramona to draw on, and a pattern. Looking at patterns was the worst part. Ramona's mother seemed to sit for hours looking at pictures of boring dresses.

At the beginning of the shopping trip, Mrs Quimby said, 'Ramona, you mustn't put your hands on things in stores.' Later she said, 'Ramona, please don't touch things.' By the time they reached the pattern counter, she said, 'Ramona, how many times do I have to tell you to keep your hands to yourself?'

When Mrs Quimby had finally selected a pattern and they were leaving the store, who should they run into but Mrs Wisser, a neighbour. 'Why, hello!' exclaimed Mrs Wisser. 'And there's Ramona! I thought a big girl like you would be going to kindergarten.'

Ramona had nothing to say.

'How old are you, dear?' asked Mrs Wisser.

Ramona still had nothing to say to Mrs Wisser, but she did hold up five fingers for the neighbour to count.

'Five!' exclaimed Mrs Wisser. 'What's the matter, dear? Has the cat got your tongue?'

Ramona stuck out her tongue just enough to show Mrs Wisser that the cat had not got it.

Mrs Wisser gasped.

'Ramona!' Mrs Quimby was thoroughly exasperated. 'I'm sorry, Mrs Wisser. Ramona seems to have forgotten her manners.' After this apology she said angrily, 'Ramona Geraldine Quimby, don't you ever let me catch you doing such a thing again!'

'But Mama,' protested Ramona, as she was dragged towards the parking lot, 'she *asked* me, and I was just showing – ' There was no use in finishing the sentence, because Mrs Quimby was not listening and she probably would not have understood if she had listened.

Mrs Quimby and Ramona returned home in time to pass the morning kindergarten straggling along the pavement with their seat-work papers to show their mothers. Ramona got down on the floor of the car so she would not be seen.

Later that afternoon Beezus brought Mary Jane home from school to play. 'How did you like kindergarten today, Ramona?' asked Mary Jane in a bright, false tone. It told Ramona all too clearly that she already knew Ramona had not gone to kindergarten.

'Why don't you shut up?' asked Ramona.

'I'll bet Henry Huggins isn't going to want to marry a girl who hasn't even finished kindergarten,' said Mary Jane.

'Oh, don't tease her,' said Beezus, who might laugh at her sister herself, but was quick to protect her from others. Ramona went outside and rode her two-wheeled, lopsided tricycle up and down the pavement for a while before she sadly removed Miss Binney's red ribbon, which she had woven through the spokes of her front wheel.

On the second morning Mrs Quimby took a dress out of Ramona's closet without a word.

Ramona spoke. 'I'm not going to school,' she said.

'Ramona, aren't you ever going back to kinder-garten?' Mrs Quimby asked wearily.

'Yes,' said Ramona.

Mrs Quimby smiled. 'Good. Let's make it today.'

Ramona reached for her playclothes. 'No. I'm going to stay away until Miss Binney forgets all about me, and then when I go back she'll think I'm somebody else.'

Mrs Quimby sighed and shook her head. 'Ramona, Miss Binney is not going to forget you.'

'Yes, she will,' insisted Ramona. 'She will if I stay away long enough.'

Some older children on the way to school shouted, 'Dropout!' as they passed the Quimbys' house. The day was a long, long one for Ramona. She drew some more seat work for herself, and afterwards there was nothing to do but wander around the house poking her tongue in the hole where her tooth was while she kept her lips shut tight.

That evening her father said, 'I miss my little girl's smiles.' Ramona managed a tight-lipped smile that did not show the gap in her teeth. Later she heard her father say something to her mother about 'this nonsense has gone on long enough,' and her mother answered with something about 'Ramona has to make up her own mind she wants to behave herself.'

Ramona despaired. Nobody understood. She wanted to behave herself. Except when banging her heels on the bedroom wall, she had always wanted to behave herself. Why couldn't people understand how she felt? She had only touched Susan's hair in the first place because it was so beautiful, and the last time – well, Susan had been so bossy she deserved to have her hair pulled.

Ramona soon discovered the other children in the neighbourhood were fascinated by her predicament. 'How come you get to stay out of school?' they asked.

'Miss Binney doesn't want me,' Ramona answered.

'Did you have fun in kindergarten today?' Mary Jane asked each day, pretending she did not know Ramona had stayed home. Ramona, who was not fooled for an instant, disdained to answer.

Henry Huggins was the one, quite unintentionally, who really frightened Ramona. One afternoon when she was pedalling her lopsided, two-wheeled tricycle up and down in front of her house, Henry came riding down the street delivering the *Journal*. He paused with one foot on the kerb in front of the Quimbys' house while he rolled a paper.

'Hi,' said Henry. 'That's quite a trike you're riding.'

'This isn't a trike,' said Ramona with dignity. 'This is my two-wheeler.'

Henry grinned and threw the paper on to the Quimbys' front steps. 'How come the truant officer doesn't make you go to school?' he asked.

'What's a truant officer?' asked Ramona.

'A man who gets after kids who don't go to school,' was Henry's careless answer, as he pedalled on down the street.

A truant officer, Ramona decided, must be something like the dog catcher who sometimes came to Glenwood School when there were too many dogs on the playground. He tried to lasso the dogs, and once when he did manage to catch an elderly overweight Bassett hound, he shut the dog in the back of his truck and drove away with it. Ramona did not want any truant officer to catch her and drive away with her, so she put her lopsided, two-wheeled tricycle into the garage and went into the house and stayed there, looking out from behind the curtains at the other children and poking her tongue into the space where her tooth used to be.

'Ramona, why do you keep making such faces?' asked Mrs Quimby in that tired voice she had been using the last day or so.

Ramona took her tongue out of the space. 'I'm not making faces,' she said. Pretty soon her grown-up tooth would come in without the tooth fairy paying a visit, and no one would ever know she had lost a tooth. She wondered what Miss Binney had done with her tooth. Thrown it away, most likely.

The next morning Ramona continued to draw rows of three pictures, circle two and cross out one, but the morning was long and lonely. Ramona was so lonely she even considered going back to kindergarten, but then she thought about Miss Binney, who did not like her any more and who might not be glad to see her. She decided she would have to wait much, much longer for Miss Binney to forget her.

'When do you think Miss Binney will forget me?' Ramona asked her mother.

Mrs Quimby kissed the top of Ramona's head. 'I doubt if she will ever forget you,' she said. 'Not ever, as long as she lives.'

The situation was hopeless. That noon Ramona was not at all hungry when she sat down to soup, a sandwich, and some carrot sticks. She bit into a carrot stick, but somehow chewing it took a long time. She stopped chewing altogether when she heard the doorbell chime. Her heart began to thump. Maybe the truant officer had finally come to get her and carry her off in the back of his truck. Maybe she should run and hide.

'Why, Howie!' Ramona heard her mother say. Feeling that she had had a close call, she went on chewing away at the carrot stick. She was safe. It was only Howie.

'Come on in, Howie,' said Mrs Quimby. 'Ramona is having her lunch. Would you like to stay for some soup and a sandwich? I can phone your mother and ask her if it's all right.'

Ramona hoped Howie would stay. She was that lonely.

'I just brought Ramona a letter.'

Ramona jumped from the table. 'A letter for me? Who's it from?' Here was the first interesting thing that had happened in days.

'I don't know,' said Howie. 'Miss Binney told me to give it to you.'

Ramona snatched the envelope from Howie, and, sure enough, there was RAMONA printed on the envelope.

'Let me read it to you,' said Mrs Quimby.

'It's *my* letter,' said Ramona, and tore open the

envelope. When she pulled out the letter, two things caught her eye at once – her tooth Scotch-taped to the top of the paper and the first line, which Ramona could read because she knew how all letters began. 'DEAR RAMONA &' was followed by two lines of printing, which Ramona was not able to read.

'Mama!' cried Ramona, filled with joy. Miss Binney had not thrown away her tooth, and Miss Binney had drawn ears and whiskers on her *Q*. The teacher liked the way Ramona made *Q*, so she must like Ramona, too. There was hope after all.

'Why, Ramona!' Mrs Quimby was astonished. 'You've lost a tooth! When did that happen?'

'At school,' said Ramona, 'and here it is!' She waved the letter at her mother, and then she studied it carefully, because she wanted so much to be able to read Miss Binney's words herself. 'It says, "Dear Ramona Q. Here is your tooth. I hope the tooth fairy brings you a dollar. I miss you and want you to come back to kindergarten. Love and kisses, Miss Binney." '

Mrs Quimby smiled and held out her hand. 'Why don't you let me read the letter?'

Ramona handed over the letter. Maybe the words did not say exactly what she had pretended to read, but she was sure they must mean the same.

' "Dear Ramona Q," ' began Mrs Quimby. And she remarked, 'Why, she makes her *Q* the same way as you do.'

'Go on, Mama,' urged Ramona, eager to hear what the letter really said.

Mrs Quimby read, ' "I am sorry I forgot to give you your tooth, but I am sure the tooth fairy will understand. When are you coming back to kindergarten?" '

Ramona did not care if the tooth fairy understood or not. Miss Binney understood and nothing else mattered. 'Tomorrow, Mama!' she cried. 'I'm going to kindergarten tomorrow!'

'Good girl!' said Mrs Quimby and hugged Ramona.

'She can't,' said matter-of-fact Howie. 'To-morrow is Saturday.'

Ramona gave Howie a look of pity, but she said, 'Please stay for lunch, Howie. It isn't tuna fish. It's peanut butter and jelly.'

WOOF!
Allan Ahlberg

Eric is a perfectly ordinary boy. Perfectly ordinary, that is, until the night when, safely tucked up in bed, he slowly turns into a dog! Fritz Wegner's drawings illustrate this funny and exciting story superbly.

VERA PRATT AND THE FALSE MOUSTACHES
Brough Girling

There were times when Wally Pratt wished his mum was more ordinary and not the fanatic mechanic she was, but when he and his friends find themselves caught up in a real 'cops and robbers' affair, he is more than glad to have his mum, Vera, to help them.

SADDLEBOTTOM
Dick King-Smith

Hilarious adventures of a Wessex Saddleback pig whose white saddle in in the wrong place, to the chagrin of his mother.

A TASTE OF BLACKBERRIES
Doris Buchanan Smith

The moving story about a young boy who has to come to terms with the tragic death of his best friend and the guilty feeling that he could somehow have saved him.

THE PRIME MINISTER'S BRAIN

Gillian Cross

The fiendish demon headmaster plans to gain control of No. 10 Downing Street and lure the Prime Minister into his evil clutches.

JASON BODGER AND THE PRIORY GHOST

Gene Kemp

A ghost story, both funny and exciting, about Jason, the bane of every teacher's life, who is pursued by the ghost of a little nun from the twelfth century!

HALFWAY ACROSS THE GALAXY AND TURN LEFT

Robin Klein

A humorous account of what happens to a family banished from their planet Zygron, when they have to spend a period of exile on Earth.

TOM TIDDLER'S GROUND

John Rowe Townsend

Vic and Brian are given an old rowing boat which leads to the unravelling of a mystery and a happy reunion of two friends. An exciting adventure story.